★★★★★★ Chester W. ★★★★★★
NIMITZ

ADMIRAL CHESTER W. NIMITZ
— *From painting by Seymour Stone, 1946. Courtesy Admiral Nimitz Center, Fredericksburg, Texas*

★★★★★★ Chester W. ★★★★★★
NIMITZ

ADMIRAL Of The Hills

With Introduction by
Ernest M. Eller, Rear Admiral USN (Ret.)

Special
Commemorative
Edition

Dede W. CASAD   **Frank A. DRISCOLL**

EAKIN PRESS ⫸ Fort Worth, Texas

DEDICATION

*To those men of the sea
who have measured up to the standards
set by John Paul Jones
over two hundred years ago —
standards epitomized by Chester W. Nimitz*

Copyright © 1983
By Dede W. Casad and Frank A. Driskill

Published in the United States of America
By Eakin Press
An Imprint of Wild Horse Media Group
P.O. Box 331779
Fort Worth, Texas 76163
www.EakinPress.com

ISBN 0-89015-364-7

All rights reserved. No part of this book may be reproduced in any form without written permission from the publisher, except for brief passages included in a review appearing in a newspaper or magazine.

TABLE OF CONTENTS

Foreword vii
Introduction ix

PART I — NIMITZ, THE BOY
  Chapter 1 An Admiral Is Born 3
  Chapter 2 A Steamboat on Dry Land 19
  Chapter 3 At the Knee of Tivy Mountain 35

PART II — NIMITZ, THE MIDSHIPMAN
  Chapter 4 Annapolis Not West Point 51
  Chapter 5 The Waves Rise Up 69
  Chapter 6 The Unexpected Charts A Course .. 83

PART III — NIMITZ, THE MAN
  Chapter 7 The Portrait of a Leader 105

PART IV — NIMITZ, THE ADMIRAL
  Chapter 8 To Sea by Train 123
  Chapter 9 Fleeting Up 135
  Chapter 10 Midway to Victory 151
  Chapter 11 The War Behind the War 167
  Chapter 12 1943 179
  Chapter 13 1944 193
  Chapter 14 1945 215

PART V — NIMITZ, THE PEACEMAKER
  Chapter 15 Cheers 233
  Chapter 16 Permission to Go Ashore 257
  Chapter 17 Old Admirals Never Retire 271

Epilogue 279
Acknowledgments 285
Bibliography 292
Index 295

CHESTER W. NIMITZ Oak and Marker in Spiegel Grove, Fremont, Ohio, home of President Rutherford B. Hayes.
— *Courtesy Admiral Nimitz State Historical Park*

FOREWORD

It seems incredible that the man who led the greatest military assemblage in world history would not have made enemies. But even the Japanese consider Admiral Nimitz to be one of the three greatest admirals, along with their Admiral Heihachiro Togo and Britain's Admiral Horatio Nelson. Nimitz's former gunnery officer, Rear Admiral E.M. Eller, said he was "the wise, calm tower of strength in adversity and success, the principal architect of victory in the Pacific." Former Nimitz staffer William H. Ewing called him "the greatest man I have ever known."

Perhaps the finest testimonial came from author James Michener: "Later I came to know Nimitz, and when I saw him in action I understood the sources from which his unusual intellectual powers came. He was a well disciplined man, but not rigid. He was willing to take a chance but was never flamboyant. He could look single facts in the eye and decide what they were worth, and he could assemble multiplex facts and make them yield a conclusion. In my life I have been fortunate in knowing a good many unusual men and women. Chester Nimitz stands at the top of the list."

I hope you will enjoy this fine story of his life.

Douglass Hubbard, Superintendent
Admiral Nimitz State Historical Park

ERNEST M. ELLER, Rear Admiral USN (Ret.) served as Admiral Nimitz's gunnery officer during much of the war. He served as U.S. Navy historian for seventeen years prior to final retirement.

INTRODUCTION

Years from now, looking back on the 20th Century, man will call it a watershed in history. When the command of this world's seas by the Royal Navy declined, so did world peace. There followed two world wars and many lesser ones that shook civilization to its foundations. In the bitter struggles of World War II the U.S. Pacific Fleet, by 1945 the mightiest navy of all time, made victory possible. This victory, in which Admiral Nimitz stands out like a beacon, could have blessed mankind for generations had Washington kept the navy strong.

This book interestingly brings out the influences on the boy Nimitz that profoundly shaped the man Nimitz and the leader. Gradually we see developing the officer that subordinates would love. He was a humble, simple man — self-effacing, yet confident and assured. He was human and down to earth, self-possessed, but not self-important. His quiet reserve radiated strength. He had a deep respect for the feelings of others, disliked open criticism, and never in my experience did he publicly criticize or tongue-lash subordinates.

He innately knew how to handle men, picking them for duty and then letting them do the job with only policy direction. As he said, a good horse pulls harder when the reins lie loose.

The admiral disliked heated dissension, as the authors well bring out. His favorite device to break the tension of strong men hotly disagreeing in conference was to interject, "This reminds me ..." Then launch into a ludicrous anecdote. Emotion would dissolve in laughter.

Admiral Nimitz expected loyalty from those under him, and he gave loyalty in return. He knew they loved our country and were as much interested in winning the war as he was. Throughout the pages hereafter readers will note those and other of his traits that so strongly shaped victory for America and freedom.

The destiny of the Pacific War lay on the admiral's shoulders, yet he did not show it. As a junior lieutenant commander, I joined his small staff in May, 1942. He was in the midst of intensive preparations for Midway, one of the crucial battles of history. Yet he took time to greet me informally and graciously in our makeshift office on the top deck of a Pearl Harbor warehouse. Frequently he called me to his office on some question. He was always business, but always polite. Even when I got into detail he didn't need — for he comprehended the core of a matter quickly — he was courteous. I soon learned he had heard all he wanted to hear when he started to shift the pencils on his desk from one spot to another — which meant "Enough."

Admiral Nimitz was habitually equable and unruffled. Even in the greatest crisis he kept his emotions under control. Thus he faced decisions of the utmost importance to the nation with a cool, clear mind. This was an important factor in his leadership of the millions of sailors, marines, and soldiers whose intrepid achievements loom large in the United States' measuring up to the demands of world leadership in World War II. Their valor and sacrifice became part of the noble heritage that weaves like a golden cord through our history. Without such a leader and such men, we would not be free today and cannot remain free.

Since the dawn of history power on the sea has shaped man's fate. The United States Navy has had a profound effect in this. It made independence possible. It has played a decisive role in every major war since. Had the navy failed in the Pacific, the United States' greatness would have ended like a comet flaming brightly, then collapsing in darkness.

It is tragic then that as soon as the war ended our government began not just to reduce but to slash beyond safety the great navy without which peace could not have been won—and without which, as Korea soon showed—it cannot keep. Our leaders forgot history. They forgot that had our fleet been stronger, Japan would not have risked Pearl Harbor, or if she had, the dedicated men in the Pacific would not have had to fight against the odds that brought such loss and suffering. They forgot the ever repeated lesson that the sea binds free nations together ... or divides them unless it is held in strength. They forgot that the obligation of the world leader of freedom is to keep strong, not least of all at sea.

Consequently a series of local wars have followed. After each, still refusing to learn, Washington let the U.S. Navy slide toward inferiority in numbers even as the Kremlin built to win the seas.

The United States has many problems besides holding the sea. Command of the Great Waters will not assure survival. Yet if she fails at sea nothing else will matter. If she fails there she fails everywhere.

> Ernest M. Eller
> Rear Admiral USN (Ret.)
> Annapolis, Maryland

DOUGLASS HUBBARD, superintendent of the Admiral Nimitz State Park in Fredericksburg, Texas, visits the shrine of Admiral Heihachiro Togo in Tokyo.
— *Courtesy Admiral Nimitz State Historical Park*

1

NIMITZ

The Boy

THE HOME OF Heinrich and Dorthea Henke on Main Street in Fredericksburg where Chester Nimitz was born.
— *Courtesy Admiral Nimitz State Historical Park*

1

An Admiral Is Born

The odds were one in a million.

For a boy from the Texas Hill Country to become commander-in-chief of the largest military armada ever assembled was about as unthought of as sending a man to the moon — and yet they both have become a part of history.

One of the first German settlements in the mid-century movement in Texas was Fredericksburg, so named in honor of Prince Friedrich of Prussia. The prince had shown sympathy for his fellow countrymen who were victims of the estate system in the homeland.

The heritage of this pioneer village was completely German and today it remains much the same. Visitors come from far and wide to enjoy the traditional food, distinctive and spicy as only natives with pride and patience can prepare it.

The German Texans had been slow to develop a bilingual society. Finally, when it did take shape, it was from necessity rather than desire. One family sent their son away to college. He wrote home explaining he would be required to take a foreign language and wanted to know what he should take. His parents talked it over and then replied: "Tak English, Son. De people haf already scharted bespeakin' it aroundt hier."

The language of the street is a mixture of German and English. Signs in some store windows declare, "English is also spoken here," an indication this small town still relates to its ancestry.

To preserve the Old World charm in a New World setting has been the goal of these descendants of 18th century German colonists. They are determined to avoid a mass-media motivated economy which would hasten change and promote growth. Visitors are welcome to enjoy the traditional lifestyle that has remained but are not encouraged to become residents of this selective community.

Heinrich and Dorthea Henke, a young couple who accompanied Baron Ottfried Hans von Meusebach from New Braunfels in 1846, became a part of the early history of Fredericksburg. It was in their home on Main Street that their oldest daughter, Anna Henke Nimitz, gave birth to her first child on February 24, 1885, a son, Chester William Nimitz.

His grandfather, Captain Charles H. Nimitz, because of his own experiences in the German merchant marine, resolved to teach his grandson early to love the sea as he always had. For patriotic reasons, Captain Nimitz liked to associate young Chester's birthday with that of George Washington. His mother, on the other hand, preferred to turn back the clock and call him "My Valentine Boy."

The two most influential people in the early life of Chester Nimitz were his mother and his paternal grandfather. Years later the Fleet Admiral wrote of his grandfather: "I didn't know my father, because he died before I was born, but I had a wonderful white-bearded grandfather. He was Charles H. Nimitz, who settled in Fredericksburg, Texas, and built a steamboat-shaped hotel. Between chores and homework I listened wide-eyed to stories about his youth in the German merchant marine. 'The sea — like life itself — is a stern taskmaster,' he would tell me. 'The best way to get along with either is to learn all you can, then do your best and don't worry — especially over things over which you have no control.'"

Although it was not a deliberate action, young Chester's early life was a conflict of wills. His mother leaned in one direction and his grandfather pulled in another. Anna Nimitz wanted her son to have the gentle qualities of his father. On the other hand Captain Nimitz instilled in his grandson that self-defense is the first law of survival and assured him that long range survival depends on the character of the individual involved.

Like other children in the area, Chester grew up in a bilingual environment. The immigrants spoke German among themselves but if strangers were present, they reluctantly shifted to English. At times they mixed the two languages if they felt the need to disguise some of their crusty side remarks.

The children liked to slip around when they thought they wouldn't be seen and listen to the men talk. As a result, they learned some choice words. They also got their mouths washed out with strong soap after they repeated those words.

Young Chester was no exception. While hiding behind the bar in the hotel saloon, listening to his grandfather tell some tall Texas tales, he was caught by his mother. She started looking for him when the call to come help her had gone unanswered. She was making bread and needed him to work the dough.

Anna Nimitz had a good idea of where to look

GRANDFATHER NIMITZ in the early days of the Steamboat Hotel.
— *Courtesy Admiral Nimitz State Historical Park*

for her four-year-old son. Amid the laughter of Captain Nimitz and his visitors, she led him away to the kitchen sputtering reprimands in German. All the while Chester was pulling away from her.

When they reached the kitchen, he relaxed. Looking up at his mother with a twinkle in his eyes, he spoke in German: *"Mutter, du hast mehl an deiner Nase!"* (You have flour on your nose, Mother.)

Anna Nimitz found it difficult to keep a straight face. Her snappy eyes softened as she put a towel over her face to cover her expression. She gave him a gentle push in the direction of the bread board and said in an attempt to remain firm, *"Machen sie sehr schnell."* (Make yourself hurry.)

The little incident marked the beginning of a pattern the future admiral would employ the rest of his life. It involved action built around patience, a sense of humor that withstood adversity, and an accurate ability to evaluate people.

In spite of his humble beginning, Chester Nimitz had an aristocratic background. The von Nimitz family migrated to Saxton, Germany, from the Baltic state of Livonia, making the move after the Thirty Years War. Sweden had taken over northern Livonia, forcing the Nimitz men to fight with the Swedish army.

The Nimitz name had long been prominent in military affairs. Their activities dated back to the Knights of the Sword where an organization called the Knights of the Teutonic Order originated. They concentrated on converting pagans to Christianity in the disputed territory between Germany and Poland. Later they took over land along the Baltic coast in an area that is now a part of Poland.

The Nimitz family seemed to take roots in Germany but it wasn't long until they were eager to be on the move again. Glowing reports about a new land, known as Texas, began to reach Germany and Poland by letters received from missionaries working in and around New Braunfels, a German village settled in 1844.

The German immigrants began arriving at ports on the Texas coast the last two months in 1844. The Nimitz family was not among the original settlers and part of them did not come to Texas at all. The first six thousand immigrants arrived at Indianola, a Gulf Coast port on Matagorda Bay, which later was destroyed by storm.

There were many hardships to overcome from Indianola to New Braunfels and the trip took about three weeks. Many of the women wore ankle-length dresses and wooden shoes which made walking difficult. At times they took turns riding in ox carts but their wide hats with flat crowns tended to get in their way.

The men found walking easier by wearing their high top boots with wool pants stuck down in them. They wore wool shirts topped by leather suspenders and vests made from leather or sheepskin. A few had Alpine hats but most of them wore high crown caps as they were more plentiful. As a whole the group appeared anything but prosperous and suited to the Texas climate. Most of their household belongings had been sold to get money for passage and food. They began their new life with the little money they had managed to save and their strong determination to find happiness in the new land.

Karl Heinrich Nimitz, Sr., the great-grandfather of Chester, served in the German merchant marine as did his son, Karl, Jr. The elder Nimitz did not go to sea from choice but because of a bad financial situation. He was the last of the Nimitz line to be

An Admiral Is Born

MAP SHOWING the German settlements in the Texas Hill Country.
— *Courtesy Admiral Nimitz State Historical Park*

blessed with a title and prosperity but the neglect of his estate caused him to go bankrupt. As a playboy, so to speak, he was inclined to hunt during the day and party at night. When there was no other recourse he settled his debts by going to sea. As soon as he was able to discharge his obligations he sought new sources of income.

In 1840 three of Karl's older children migrated to Charleston, South Carolina. He and their mother joined them three years later after he had given up the sea. Karl, Jr. followed about a year later and the Nimitz family was united once more.

Karl, Jr. was unable to adjust to the quiet life in Charleston after his years at sea. He had heard of other German immigrants going to Texas so he decided to explore what might be found farther west. He sailed down the Atlantic coast into the Gulf of Mexico and landed at Indianola. From here he made the trip to New Braunfels. Baron von Meusebach was ready to leave there for his pioneer journey into the Texas Hill Country, so the admiral's grandfather joined the group that founded Fredericksburg.

When the new settlement was established and chartered many of the immigrants anglicized their Christian names. Baron Ottfried Hans von Meusebach became John O. Meusebach. The admiral's grandfather changed his name from Karl Heinrich Nimitz to Charles Henry Nimitz.

In 1848, two years after Fredericksburg was founded, Charles Henry Nimitz married Sophie Dorthea Muller, the daughter of a fellow settler. The next year she presented him with the first of twelve children.

There are conflicting reports concerning the first years of married life for the grandparents of Chester Nimitz. One account has Charles keeping books for a lumber company situated on the nearby Pedernales River. Another credits the couple with being cooks at Fort Martin Scott, one of several army posts set up to protect the settlers from roving bands of Indians. A third report mentions Charles serving briefly with the Texas Rangers, the elite law enforcement organization.

The records at the Texas Capitol in Austin give no indication that a Charles Henry Nimitz was ever a member but records then were not complete. It is difficult to know whether he served or not.

His true profession surfaced in 1852 when he built a small hotel near the east end of Main Street to accommodate ranchers, the soldiers, and the sales people who came that way. It was an immedi-

BARON MEUSEBACH, who renounced his title in Germany, to become John O. Meusebach, the leader of early colonists in Texas. Admiral Nimitz's grandfather became a part of Meusebach's colony in Fredericksburg.
— *Photo provided by Mrs. Irene Marschall King, Wago, Texas, from copy at U.S. Institute of Texan Cultures.*

ate success since it was the only place for travelers moving westward to stay between Indianola and San Diego, California. Later, El Paso was established but Fredericksburg still was the first stop.

Charles Nimitz decided to expand and built the new structure in the shape of a Mississippi River steamboat, complete with a superstructure, a mast, and a crow's nest. This unusual design was a reflection of his earlier love for the sea. In later years he would sit in the crow's nest and hold his grandson, as they looked down on the main street. Here many of his early experiences were related. According to reliable reports, many of his sea stories originated in that same crow's nest.

An expansion program enlarged the original structure from a "six room adobe house" to a hotel with forty-five guest rooms, a dining room, a saloon, and a combination ballroom and theater. In the rear was a smokehouse, a brewery, and a bathhouse, the first on the frontier. All the facilities of the Steamboat Hotel were surrounded by an adobe wall which was topped by broken glass for protection from thieving Indians.

The maternal grandparents of the future admiral settled further north on Main Street. Heinrich Henke, a teamster who hauled freight for the Confederate forces, also opened the first meat market in Fredericksburg. After processing the fresh meat in the back yard, he sold it from the front porch of the little fieldstone house. The horses that pulled the wagon used for home delivery were also stabled in the back yard.

In time a long dining room and kitchen, covered by a slanting roof, were added to accommodate the growing Henke family which finally totaled twelve children. It is interesting to note that both of Chester Nimitz's parents came from families with twelve

ANNA NIMITZ, the attractive mother of Chester W. Nimitz.
— *Courtesy Admiral Nimitz State Historical Park*

children. His father was the third child in the Charles Nimitz family while his mother was the oldest of the Henke children. It was thought by some that the marriage of Charles Bernard Nimitz and Anna Henke should not have taken place but the history of the world was changed when their son became an admiral.

Only four sons of Charles Nimitz lived to maturity. Chester Bernard Nimitz was the one who was entirely different from his dynamic father. With clear blue eyes and soft blond hair, he had the look of a minister, a teacher, or perhaps a poet. He was frail with weak lungs and a rheumatic heart. To try to improve his health, Chester became a drover and joined cattle drives from Texas into Nebraska.

Doctors advised Chester not to marry but this did not keep him from falling in love with Anna Henke. Anna was a classic beauty but she had a strong determination like her father. Her help with the upbringing of her brothers and sisters had made her accustomed to responsibility. Her popularity as a young girl was supported by her many suitors but she accepted the proposal of bashful young Chester Nimitz. They were married in March 1884 when he was twenty-nine and she was in her early twenties. Five months later Anna Nimitz was left pregnant and a widow.

After his son's death, Captain Nimitz was quick to move Anna and his grandson into the hotel. Their presence was a welcome diversion since he, too, had recently been widowed.

By then, Charles Henry, Jr., his second son, was doing much of the work in managing the hotel. William, the youngest boy, was in Massachusetts attending Worcester Polytechnic Institute. He became the only one of the Nimitz boys to receive a college education.

There was no demand for engineers in Fredericksburg and William spent his time watching the simple construction that was taking place downtown or else talking to the guests at the hotel. His father had some misgivings about his investment.

"*Ach, mein Gott im Himmel,*" the captain would frequently say. "I put store-bought clothes on that boy and sent him where he could learn how to do better in life. All it did was ruin a damn good deck hand."

An Admiral Is Born   15

HEINRICH and DORTHEA Henke, grandparents of Chester Nimitz.

— *Courtesy Admiral Nimitz State Historical Park*

While still a baby, Chester was christened into the Zion Lutheran Church in Fredericksburg but the captain had his own ideas about where the ceremony should take place. From the day his grandson was born he had planned to have it take place at the Steamboat Hotel — "where it should be."

The ballroom at the hotel was filled. Town people were joined by visitors in for the occasion. Several lieutenants, resplendent in their army blues, were en route to new assignments and attended the occasion. Their fondness for the captain caused them to suggest "what a fine army officer young Chester would make."

The remarks fell on deaf ears. The presence of army brass didn't slow the captain down at all. When the Lutheran pastor had performed the regular ceremony, the proud *"Opa"* had one of his own. It was at that moment that the captain decided to teach his first grandson to use the German words in referring to his grandparents. *"Opa"* and *"Oma"* had a more intimate appeal to him — and besides that's the way he wanted it.

Opa Nimitz turned and faced those in the ballroom: "To a future admiral in the United States Navy — my grandson," he called out in a loud voice as he held his beer glass high. Later, after the activity had moved to the saloon, he bought a round of drinks — individual choice — and directed an even louder toast to the friendly lieutenants. There could be no mistaking his meaning.

Perhaps it was an omen of things to come, who knows? If so, it remained well hidden for nearly two decades.

Charles Nimitz's experiences at sea caused some confusion about his rank as "captain." It was assumed by many visitors that it was a navy title but this was not true. It was an army rating he had earned as captain of the Gillespie Rifles. This was a company of volunteers organized to protect the settlers from Indian raids when Union troops had been recalled after the outbreak of the Civil War. During the time Chester was growing up, *Opa* didn't bother to correct those who thought he was a navy captain. He even let the children who came to listen to his stories think he had been a sea captain.

The neighborhood children loved Chester's grandfather and he loved them. Besides an ever-growing list of stories that held their attention he performed card tricks that kept them coming back for more.

Opa also had a sure cure for children who came to him with small hurts that developed while they were scuffling. He would call them over to stand between his knees. "It doesn't hurt any more, does it?" he would ask.

He would quickly be assured that it still hurt very much. The captain would then take a nickel

LISETTA MUELLER (left), was present at the birth of Chester W. Nimitz; Miss Susan Moore (right), who taught Chester Nimitz at Tivy High School in Keerville.
— *Photos loaned by Mr. and Mrs. O. Morris*

from his pocket and show it to the injured child. "Where does it hurt?" he would ask.

After the spot was pointed out, he would put the nickel over the place in question. "Here, you hold this nickel over your hurt spot. When it stops hurting you can take the nickel off and go to the candy store."

Recovery was usually quick and with a smile.

Opa Nimitz also practiced some dentistry, without the benefit of a license. He did a flourishing business among children who were willing to trade a loose tooth for a piece of licorice. He usually had them standing in line but occasionally he found one who had to be coaxed.

He would wait until a tooth was just hanging

before he started. He would tie a piece of sewing thread around the tooth and twist it tight. While he was in the middle of one of his sea stories and the child listened with an open mouth, he would suddenly give the thread a jerk. The tooth would come out without the owner being aware of it.

To his credit, the captain did not arouse the anger of parents by spreading the story of the tooth fairy, even though he was tempted to on more than one occasion. Instead, he kept a generous supply of licorice hidden under his bed to take care of any sudden increase in business.

As time passed Captain Nimitz began to feel the need to curtail his story-telling activity. His own grandchildren increased in number — as did their friends in the neighborhood. He found it more difficult to have a fresh supply of experiences available. Finally, he explained that he could never make another voyage on a ship.

"I turned my back on the sea," he told them, "and when you do that you will not be allowed to use the ocean again. If you do, the sea will swallow you up as punishment."

Later, when he had forgotten the story he told he took a boat trip to New York. The children at home were beside themselves for fear he would be swallowed up by the sea before he could return.

They immediately questioned him when he got back to see how he had managed to keep from being punished.

"I begged forgiveness," he told them. "I promised to make amends. I promised to give the sea one of my own grandsons — as an admiral."

2

A Steamboat on Dry Land

As a young boy growing up, Chester Nimitz had no desire to go to sea, in spite of his grandfather's stories; but he was the first youngster in Fredericksburg to get a "crewcut."

Both of his parents had deep blue eyes and Nordic blond hair so it was natural for Chester to be towheaded. It was also natural for guests at the hotel who didn't know his name to call him "cottontop." Chester didn't mind his blue eyes but until his hair became dark enough to get him out of the cottontop class, he resented the teasing moniker.

One day when one of the men jovially referred to him as "cottontop," Chester leaned forward and kicked him on the shin with all the strength a three year old could muster. His mother dutifully punished him with a quick spanking and a sharp reprimand. The punishment for expressing himself was, Chester thought, unfair and uncalled for. He decided to revenge the corrective measure so he headed out back.

The solution seemed to be in a bucket of green

EARLY PHOTOGRAPH of the Steamboat Hotel in Fredericksburg.
— *Courtesy Admiral Nimitz State Historical Park*

paint. The can had been resealed and put in a closet on a shelf but Chester was able to get it down. He then slipped into the smokehouse without being seen.

His hair was a solid mass of green when he came out. "They won't call me a 'cottontop' any more," he said to himself as he sat in the shade of the bathhouse to let the paint dry.

His mother was horrified when she saw him but his grandfather picked up the humor in the act. "He's a Nimitz," the old captain said, "hellbent on showing folks what he has on his mind."

Ordinary home scissors would not cut through the thick mat of paint and hair. Anna Nimitz had to use sheep shears and even then the task wasn't easy. When she finished the green paint was gone but so was most of her son's hair.

As soon as his hair grew out, she had a new picture made. His blonde hair was her pride and joy and she wanted to have his new look to cherish.

Anna Nimitz let it be known her son was not to be called a "cottontop" any more. Those involved spent time in the saloon and to avoid the wrath of his pretty daughter-in-law, the old captain saw to it that they got the message.

Young Chester never questioned anything his grandfather did or said as he trusted his judgment completely. He didn't even say anything about the little derby hat the captain gave him to wear to school. It didn't seem to fit in with his other clothes. He was barefooted and wore only a shirt and short pants held up by suspenders. As soon as he got to school the derby was knocked off his head. Then three boys played "keep away" until Chester finally got it back. It was knocked off again and several fights followed. When he got home from school both eyes were black, his lip was split, and his clothes were torn. The brim of the hat was barely attached to the crown but he held it proudly in his hand. "I took my hat to school," he told his *Opa*, "and I brought it home."

Although there was no resentment over the incident, Chester frequently wondered why *Opa* had put him in such a position. Although he used the term "grandfather" when he was talking to a stranger, Chester had started using *Opa* and *Oma* as the captain had planned.

Even after he became commander of the Pacific Theatre, Chester thought about the derby incident. He liked to think it was a way to make him realize he must always be in a position to defend himself — something his proud grandfather had continued to point out to him. There were some, however, who thought the old man could not resist a good prank, even if it were on his grandson.

Chester never felt that way and an incident a few years later led him to believe he was right. It happened on a return visit to Fredericksburg after he had moved to Kerrville with his mother and stepfather. He was about ten years old at the time.

One afternoon Chester complained to his grandfather that a boy kept trying "to run over him." When the old man heard the name of the boy he exclaimed: "Why he isn't any bigger than you are! You go look him up for a change — and you fight him. Not only do you fight him but you whip him. Do that and he'll stop picking on you."

"When do I have to go?" Chester asked rather timidly.

"Anytime before you eat," his grandfather replied.

Chester ran down the alley before he lost his nerve and saw the boy in question talking to another boy. It was now or never. Without saying anything Chester walked up and started punching away at him. Taken by surprise the boy took a good

CHESTER NIMITZ, taken after his hair had grown out after his "crew cut."
— *Courtesy Admiral Nimitz State Historical Park*

whipping. After that, he offered to shake hands and Chester accepted the offer.

When Chester went to the hotel for supper his grandfather was waiting for him. "Are you ready to eat?" he asked.

When he replied, "Yes, sir," a proud *Opa* handed him his plate.

That same summer the old captain passed on some philosophy that the admiral recalled many times during the dark days in the Pacific. Looking back on his association with his grandfather, he marveled at the depth of meaning most of his statements had. For a man who had gone to sea as a young boy with an education that was acquired mostly through the trial and error method, he presented a knowledge more profound than that of many with much more formal education.

Chester went to his grandfather and complained that his cousin, Karl, who was two years older, was avoiding him. "Karl and his friends think I am too little to go around with them. What do I do?"

The advice was short and to the point. "Get used to it. They will always be two years older than you are. What you cannot change you must get used to."

Chester started to walk away when the captain called him back. "Wait a minute, son," he said. "I need to explain a little more."

He brought Chester over where he would be standing by his knee, a position the old captain liked to use when he was talking to young boys. "You will need to learn the difference between things that will never change and things time will take care of. Now the difference between your age and Karl's age will never change. There will always be two years difference no matter how old you are. What time will do is reach a point where the difference doesn't matter. It may make a difference now but when you are older it will not be important. Time will work on your side if you have the patience to let it take over."

Fredericksburg was about forty years old when young Chester was born. By then the concern over roving bands of Indians was gone but their activity in the past was still talked about.

Captain Nimitz mixed Indian stories with his yarns about the sea. It was he who first told Chester about the legend of the Easter Fires. He could speak with authority since he lived there when the observance began.

Fredericksburg had been laid out on the edge of the Comanche hunting grounds so Baron von Meusebach negotiated a treaty with the chief of the Indian tribes. He agreed that the white settlers would stay away from areas the Indians felt belonged to them. The treaty was honored but not without concern by both parties.

The settlers had heard about the "Comanche Moon." Legend has it that the first full moon in September brought a change in the lives of the Indians. They gave up their quiet life when they hunted and fished and took to one that caused them to roam and plunder and kill. In September, war parties moved from the Texas Panhandle to the north, through an area known as the Great Comanche war trail, west of Fort Concho, on through the now extinct village of Las Moras into Mexico. Fort Concho was located a few miles from what is now San Angelo, on the Concho River, a tributary of the Colorado. The Colorado River swings east of Fredericksburg, through Austin, and on to the Gulf of Mexico.

A series of outposts — or forts — helped to protect the settlers who had moved farther west. It was in this area that the legend of the Easter Fires

FREDERICKSBURG, Texas at the turn of the century.
— *Courtesy Admiral Nimitz State Historical Park*

originated, the hills just west of Fredericksburg.

September war parties were of some concern to the settlers although they never actually came into the village as a raiding party. They did slip in and steal when they could so it was natural for the settlers not to completely trust the Indians' treaty.

The Comanches had misgivings of their own. The white man had broken so many treaties in the past the Indians needed to be more assured. According to the legend, the Indians took precautions by building signal fires on the hills overlooking the town. As long as the fires blazed, the braves in distant camps knew all was well.

The children of the German settlers were frightened until a mother invented a story to put them at ease. She told them it was the Easter rabbit at work boiling eggs in large vats and coloring them with the stain of wild berries from the hills.

The Easter Fires was one of young Chester's favorite stories. The custom of the annual fires continued, as it does today, and was reenacted by descendants of the original settlers. As a result, the old captain was able to present a realistic picture each time he told it.

During the early years when Indians could be a problem, the settlers had other signals to follow. Late in the day when a blanket of silence covered the hills and dipped into the valleys the approaching darkness would soon follow. The stillness of the night brought uncertainty until a benediction was pronounced by the sounds of the crickets and the tree frogs. The little sentinels of nature remained silent when the Indians were moving around.

By the turn of the century the Steamboat Hotel in Fredericksburg was a landmark and its owner, Captain Charles Nimitz, was a well-known personality. His stories continued to grow and his pranks brought anticipation from those who had been there before and concern from newcomers who did not know what to expect.

A favorite prank of his was the "double killing." It was set up at the bar where two "strangers" would go for their guns after a heated argument. The crowd, which was a part of the window dressing, would move back to give them room and Captain Nimitz, the bartender, always managed to be in the storeroom when the "shooting" took place. The two bodies, destined to come to rest in boot hill, always produced a lot of laughs when they suddenly became alive again.

Most of the guests who witnessed the farce took their involvement good-naturedly. "We might as well," one salesman noted. "If we take exception to what the captain does, what good will it do — besides there ain't no other place to stay."

The captain used another line of reasoning. "When folks stay here at the Steamboat, it is like they were taking a sea voyage. When they come here for the first time, it is the same as if they are crossing the equator and they have to be initiated."

He had another initiation he reserved for "greenhorns" from the East. "We will be hunting chaparral birds," he would tell them. "We call them roadrunners around here because they have long legs and long tails, and about the only time they are seen is when they run along the road, or from one side to the other. The only time they can be caught is at night and folks will pay good money for them."

The captain was very careful to explain further. "The way we catch them is to go back up in the hills where they roost at night. We take a gunny sack — you probably don't know what that is but it is a loosely woven sack that feed comes in — and we get a helper to hold the sack in the right place so when the birds are driven in the corner they will run into it. If you will hold the sack, we will spread out and drive them in. We'll follow on behind and help you carry the birds back to the hotel."

Most of the strangers didn't relish the idea of being up in the hills alone on a dark night but in an effort to be a good sport, they would agree to help out. The noises of the night, especially the unfamiliar cry of the hoot owl, caused all kinds of uneasiness and made the time drag by. Finally, when it was evident no one was coming, the trip back to the hotel added fear to the deceptive venture. Sometimes it took most of the night.

The captain, who likely had been in bed for several hours, greeted the guest when he arrived, frequently chilled to the bone and frightened from the experience. "You are now one of the Steamboat's deck crew," Charles Nimitz would tell him. "Come to the bar and I'll get you a big shot of whiskey. You can go back home and tell them you passed your tests. You aren't a greenhorn any more."

In spite of his playful attitude and his wild stories that were almost unbelievable, Charles Nimitz was well liked by his fellow citizens. He was elected to the Fredericksburg School Board and in 1891, when Chester was only six years old, he became a member of the Texas legislature in Austin. The only time he fell out of favor with his townfolk was during the Civil War. As captain of the Gillespie Rifles, he was asked to recruit for the Confederate army. Since most of the sympathy among the people in Fredericksburg was with the Union, his efforts didn't set well with them. As time passed, however, the breach was mended.

At the Steamboat Hotel, Charles Nimitz was completely in charge of the situation. An affable host, he liked people and had a way of making indi-

MAIN STREET, Fredericksburg, Texas that young Chester surveyed from the "crow's nest" at the Steamboat Hotel, with his grandfather.
— *Courtesy Admiral Nimitz State Historical Park*

vidual guests feel welcomed. The guest register, which has been preserved, lists quite a few well-known people. Many of the guests were military men going to and from their posts. One of the officers who visited frequently was Robert E. Lee who had two tours of duty in Texas before he cast his lot with the Confederate forces. He and Captain Nimitz visited frequently together. The captain usually assigned him the same room and when the war was over, he named it the "General Lee Room."

Colonel Lee appreciated the courtesies extended him when he visited Fredericksburg while he was en route to and from Fort Mason, some forty miles away. He wrote his family back in Virginia about his German friend who had "built" a steamboat in the Texas hills and used it as a hotel.

One guest of interest was O. Henry, an author from nearby Austin, who used the hotel as a model in the story, "A Chaparral Prince." Philip Sheridan, who was doing a tour of duty in Texas, and James Longstreet, also stationed at one of the outlying forts, were also frequent guests. Like Lee, both Sheridan and Longstreet became generals and Sheridan returned to Fredericksburg after the war.

The sculptress, Elizabet Ney, who settled in Austin, stayed in the hotel a few days. The records show that on March 4, 1873, an E. Roosevelt was registered but there is no further information on the identity of the owner of this famous name. Many other names of merit are shown on the register with some likely ficticious and put there as a joke to create interest.

The Christmas season was the highlight of Fredericksburg's social year. What was considered by many to be the first community Christmas tree in Texas was set up in the lobby of the Steamboat Hotel by the captain while Chester was a small boy.

A large *tannenbaum* that nearly reached the ceiling was brought in from the nearby hills. The distinctive smell of the cedar gave a holiday atmosphere to the entire front part of the hotel. Chester was underfoot the entire time the tree was being decorated and if he could have had his way, he would have gone with his *Opa* to get it.

Trimming the tree was a community project. Townsfolk brought homemade ornaments, strings of berries, paper chains made in bright colors, and strings of popped corn. The customs brought from the old country turned the little village into a panorama of enticing smells, haunting music, and community parties.

All year young Chester looked forward to this occasion. He loved his Grandmother Henke's anise cookies and enjoyed hearing his mother sing *Stille Nacht* at the church. He especially liked to listen to the singers who would gather at the community building — *the Vereins Kirche* — to sing Christmas carols. He always thought his mother was the prettiest lady there and had the best voice.

Oma Henke's anise cookies were kept in a jar since Chester and his friends couldn't resist pinching little pieces off of those they could reach hanging from the tree.

The captain liked to tell the story of Christmas. He said the celebration of Christmas and the use of the *tannenbaum* began in Germany and was only perfected and expanded in America. Everyone believed him.

"Even the story of Santa Claus originated in Germany," he told them, "only then his name was Kris Kringle. All the children waited anxiously for his coming each year. He would bring them candy and fruit and a toy for their stockings they hung by the chimney. But old Kris Kringle had to change his name, like I did, when he came to this new world. Over there my name was Karl. Here it is Charles. And over here Kris Kringle is called Santa Claus."

The Steamboat Hotel was the center of activity during the Christmas season. The gala occasion rivaled the activity in nearby San Antonio. Since the Civil War, Fredericksburg had been designated as a stage stop on the regular run to El Paso and army officers used the hotel as a rest stop for their families when members were going to and from their designated posts. The number of "drummers" or salesmen increased with the availability of stage travel and some of them stayed over for Christmas. Captain Nimitz had an oasis in the wide open spaces and he took advantage of it.

The love for music by the German settlers was never more evident than at Christmas time. Anytime a few people got together instruments of some kind — usually accordions — were always in evidence. Most of the men could play and since they usually played by ear it didn't matter whether the words were written in German or English.

There were always two or three dances during the holiday season and the area military people were invited. Most of the troops at the outlying forts were black so there was no problem in separating the officers from the enlisted men.

With *wurst* (sausage) and beer available in large quantities and a local group to provide the music, the ballroom was always filled and overflowing. Older people, frequently not able to dance, sat around the walls and kept time with the music. The children were not allowed to come in to the dance but attended the festivities and played out in front of the hotel or in the lobby around the Christmas tree.

Officers from other parts of the United States had to learn to dance the polka and the schottisches but it didn't take them long. The townsfolk were anxious to teach them. Young girls especially made an effort to dance with the men in blue, many of whom had not been out of the Academy long. It was in the ballroom at the Steamboat Hotel in Fredericksburg at Christmas time that more than one budding career officer met his *fraulein* whom he later married.

3

At The Knee of Tivy Mountain

It was during such a happy holiday season that Chester Nimitz gained a new father. On Christmas Day in 1890, Anna Nimitz married William Nimitz — "Uncle Willie" to Chester — in a joyous ceremony at the Steamboat Hotel. While other children were receiving Christmas gifts, Chester received a new father without having to change his name.

When the youngest son of Captain Charles Nimitz won the hand of Anna, his widowed sister-in-law who was twenty-nine and still a beauty, the people in the community were pleased. The captain was especially pleased because he felt the responsibility of a wife and child might give his irresponsible son a purpose in life that had been missing.

William Nimitz had to be classified as an educated ne'er-do-well. The college degree he received in Massachusetts made him the best educated man in town but unfortunately there was no demand for a professional engineer in Fredericksburg. After his marriage to Anna, there appeared little possibility for work until an older widowed sister offered him a job as the manager of the St. Charles Hotel in nearby Kerrville.

About all Anna accomplished in the twenty-five mile move was changing from one hotel to another. It helped some that the kitchen at the St. Charles was smaller and the dining room would not seat as many people. It wasn't long until it was evident that she had made another unfortunate marriage.

"*Nach Gottes willen,*"—according to God's will —was the expression Anna used to explain the sitution and patiently made the best of it.

Anna did much of the work at the hotel. She was in charge of the dining room and kitchen, and filled in at the front desk when she was needed. When Chester reached high school, he helped some in the afternoon since William was away much of the time following his nonpaying profession—downtown sidewalk engineering.

The St. Charles was little more than a glorified boarding house. It was a two-story white wooden structure, surrounded by porches and with enough bric-a-brac to distinguish it from the other buildings in the little town.

In spite of her busy life, Anna gave birth to two more children. Dora was born in 1895 and Otto came two years later. Dora and Chester were as close as a brother and sister could be in spite of the ten-year difference in their ages. He called her his "three-quarter sister" since they had the same mother and her father was his uncle, as well as his stepfather. It was Dora's appreciation of her older brother that may have saved his navy career.

Otto was only three years old when Chester went away to school so they did not see much of each other. When Otto also finished the Naval Academy their paths crossed occasionally.

Although Anna would never admit it, Chester

seemed to be her favorite child. Perhaps this was because he was her first. It could have been because he was the son of a man she had loved but had been able to live with such a short time. Whatever the reason it was something both the mother and son felt. She had called him "My Valentine Boy" when he was born and this was the last thing she said before she died. In 1925 when Chester was on maneuvers in the Pacific he received word that his mother was seriously ill. He rushed to her bedside and arrived just before she expired. As she was slipping away, she smiled and whispered: "I knew my Valentine Boy would come to see me."

In the beginning Chester was not as happy in Kerrville as he would have liked to be but he made the most of it. Perhaps without realizing it he had accepted his mother's philosophy — *"Nach Gottes willen."* He tried not to compare the St. Charles with the Steamboat but inadvertently he did anyway. It was only because he was able to make trips back to Fredericksburg in the summer and during the Christmas season that he was content at all.

Anna Nimitz was afraid her son might have inherited some of his real father's physical weaknesses so she was glad for him to spend as much time out in the open as possible. She encouraged him to run and to get plenty of exercise. Rabbit hunting was one of his favorite sports and trying to catch them made a good runner out of him. He liked to run and soon developed strong legs, good lungs, and a sturdy body. Nevertheless he had a tendency to contract pneumonia, which he did on several occasions.

The area around Kerrville and Fredericksburg was open country. Small game was plentiful and fishing in the clear, rock bottom rivers was excellent. There were many deer and wild turkey but the Nimitz men were not avid game hunters.

Frequently the captain took Chester and a friend on camping trips. They used a covered wagon in case it rained and to protect their provisions against predatory animals. It was on one of these outings that Chester had his first taste of rattlesnake. "I caught a fish while you boys were gone," the captain told them, "and I cut it up in little pieces and fried it brown."

When they finished eating and had told him how good the fish was, he let them in on his secret. "I didn't fool you just to pull a prank," he told him. "You may have to eat rattlesnake sometime and I want you to know it won't hurt you."

"Rattlesnakes are a lot like eels and you may have to eat an eel when you go to sea. Eels won't hurt you either and like rattlesnake they taste better than they look. It is good that you have found this out early."

Chester had to admit the rattlesnake tasted good but the idea didn't appeal to him. He was sure he wouldn't have tasted it if he had known what it was. Unless it was a last resort effort he knew he wouldn't try it again.

Rattlesnakes were plentiful on Grandpa Henke's ranch near Fredericksburg and Chester and his friends killed hundreds of them in the summer when they helped bale hay. The skins were valuable for belts and hatbands but the teeth of the rakes punched so many holes in the reptiles that the skins were not worth saving. The boys threw the snakes away after they cut the rattlers off. These they strung on a long wire to frighten the younger children.

As time passed Chester began to like Kerrville better. He made many friends among the boys and by the time he had entered high school he had begun to notice the girls. Even then it took a special occasion to get him involved. On one of these occasions

At the Knee of Tivy Mountain   39

he made his first amphibious landing, as Louis Schreiner called it, in a borrowed boat.

Chester was trying to impress Bertha Riley, a new girl in town. They were walking along the river after school, when he should have been at the hotel helping his mother. It was then he found the small boat Louis Schreiner had hidden under a pile of brush in the edge of the woods.

Anna Nimitz needed Chester to help her and started out to look for him. As usual she had a good idea where to look. She and Louis Schreiner met on the river bank just as Chester and Bertha came around a bend in the river paddling the boat. The Schreiner account left the impression that Anna did some paddling of her own but Dora, Chester's sister, denies it. "I never knew our mother to lay a hand on Chester," she said in an interview in 1980, not long before she died. She was probably correct but Louis Schreiner had his fun, especially when Chester returned as an admiral in the United States Navy.

As Chester grew older he became involved in an increasing number of fist fights. He didn't start them but they seemed to come his way.

"I don't think Chester ever picked a fight," Dora said in the interview, "but he never ran from one either. And if he ever lost one, I don't remember it. He would come home with his lips cut and be scratched up but it didn't seem to bother him. When Mama would say anything he would shrug it off by saying: 'You ought to see the other fellow.' Mama would just shudder but she wouldn't say anything more because she knew it wouldn't do any good.

"One time these twin brothers stopped Chester downtown and jumped on him. He whipped them both and sent them runnin'. It wasn't long until all the boys — the big ones too — began to leave him alone. By then some of them were callin' him the

'King of the Mountain.' Since no one decided to dispute it, I guess he was," she added.

Chester's close association with his mother caused him to appreciate older women. Even as a teen-age boy he attracted their attention. "He brings out the mother instinct in them," Anna told a friend. "His papa was the same way."

A spinster member of a pioneer Kerrville family was one of the ladies who called on Chester for help. She was Suson Tivy, the sister of Captain Joseph Tivy, who had served in the Confederate navy and was the first mayor of Kerrville. Captain Tivy gave a hundred acres of land on which to build the first school in the town which he helped to charter and the school still carries his name—Tivy High School. The tallest mountain, south and east of Kerrville, is also known as Tivy Mountain.

Miss Tivy lived alone near the St. Charles Hotel with her white tomcat, Herman. When he died it nearly broke her heart.

"I need your help," she told Chester. "I had a real nice coffin made several years ago but I can't stand to put Herman away. He is fifteen years old but I'm still not ready to give him up."

Chester promised to find a place where Herman would not be disturbed. He had already thought of the Tivy cemetery plot which he had seen frequently when he hunted rabbits. It was located on the side of the mountain near an abandoned outpost that had been used to observe Indian activity. The mountain was so high that on a clear day an observer looking out from the cemetery could see almost into the next county.

There were three grave sites laid out when Chester buried Herman. Captain Tivy and one sister were already interred there and the third spot had

THE PRIVATE TIVY CEMETERY on Tivy Mountain where young Chester buried "Feline Tivy." Insert shows grave marker for the pet.

— *Courtesy Kerrville Daily Times*

been left for Suson. The entire plot was marked off by large stones anchored in the ground.

Miss Tivy was surprised but pleased when Chester told her where he had taken Herman. "Why not?" Chester asked. "Herman is part of the family and belongs there."

Miss Tivy kissed him on the cheek and gave him a large piece of fresh apple strudel. Later he cut out a marker from a new piece of wood and burned the words "Feline Tivy" across the top. Underneath that he added the name "Herman."

Herman's grave is still there on Tivy Mountain. The wooden marker has been replaced by a concrete cover with only the words "Feline Tivy" and an outline drawing of a cat on it. The three graves have a single eight-foot high marker showing that Suson Tivy died in 1901, the year Chester enrolled in the U.S. Naval Academy. The entire plot, including Herman's grave, is enclosed by an iron picket fence.

When Chester was fifteen he went to work for his aunt in the hotel. He split kindling after school and filled the wood boxes. He then tended the stoves and fireplaces, if it was that time of year, and raked leaves when necessary. After supper he worked at the front desk until it closed at ten o'clock. For his efforts his aunt gave him board and room, and fifteen dollars a month.

Chester did not always have time to study while he worked at the desk at night. Since he made excellent grades he felt the necessity of getting up early in the morning to complete his assignments. Like all young boys Chester did not enjoy getting up early but grades were important to him — especially if he was to figure out a way to go to college.

With the fifteen dollars Chester received for working at the hotel, he bought his clothes, his school books, and was able to help his mother with some of her needs. It also made him feel good to be able to occasionally buy Dora and Otto surprises they might not get otherwise.

Helping his family was nothing new for Chester. When he was eight years old he earned a dollar a week working at the local meat market. This amount was increased when he started helping make deliveries. He had been around his Grandfather Henke's market in Fredericksburg enough to know what to do.

Besides the money, the butcher gave Chester

beef liver and soup bones. There hadn't been much demand for liver until Anna Nimitz started preparing it with onions and spices. The word soon spread and the local people began coming to the hotel for lunch on the days liver was served.

The large pots of beef and vegetable soup were also in demand — especially on cold days. Even the butcher who supplied the bones would drop by occasionally to sample it. Anna Nimitz had the ability to take almost anything available and make something tasty with it.

Chester was small for his age and this frequently misled people. When he was twelve, three men from San Antonio came to Kerrville to go fishing. The man hired to cook for them was sick when they arrived and they didn't know what to do.

"Take me," Chester told them. "My grandfather has taught me how to fry fish a way I know you will like."

The men were skeptical but when they couldn't find anyone else, they took Chester. It didn't take long for them to realize he knew what he was doing. He took fillets from the larger fish and the smaller ones he cut grooves on each side to prevent curling when he fried them. The men responded by giving him more money than they had promised and enough fish to serve for lunch at the hotel.

Many of the hotel guests interested Chester. Like his grandfather, he enjoyed people. As a small boy he had found out it is possible to learn by listening to traveling men from other areas. There were two traveling men — drummers — from San Antonio that he especially liked.

Sam Miller and Carl Pickard looked the part. They brought their sample merchandise in large trunks which were transported on flatbed drays, pulled by two horses. They brought their own drivers who also handled the trunks. Back of the front seat was a tent-like enclosure for protection from the elements and to sleep under at night. With hotels only in Fredericksburg and Kerrville the salesmen had to be self-sufficient most of the time.

The St. Charles had what was known as a "sample" room in the back. Here the drummers set up their trunks and displayed their merchandise at least twice and sometimes three times a year. Merchants from Kerrville and country stores in the outlying areas came to make their selection and place orders.

Chester looked forward to the visits because Miller and Pickard usually came by Fredericksburg before they reached Kerrville. They always had messages from the family there and often they had packages for the entire family from Grandfather Nimitz.

Chester began to think more about how he would continue his education. He knew from experience that he didn't want to run a meat market or manage a hotel. The wanderlust he had inherited from his grandfather was too strong to be denied. There were some things about being a drummer that appealed to him but the uncertainty of selling caused him concern. Although his drummer friends encouraged him to try it when he got out of school, Chester didn't think he was cut out to be a salesman.

When the opportunity presented itself, Chester would discuss his future with his grandfather. They always seemed to return to philosophy — with question marks. Chester had a curiosity that seemed to demand answers that were not readily available. The questions were simple but the answers depended on a series of unknowns. They talked about luck and fate and destiny. Then they discussed how some people seemed to get the "breaks" and others were not so fortunate.

"I have always believed that people make their

At the Knee of Tivy Mountain 45

own breaks," the old man frequently said. "Just how, I'm not sure. Maybe it's through the mistakes of others and maybe it is from good planning. Part of it had to be planning, I know. When you go to sea you will need to know how to plan carefully." The white beard seemed to stiffen as the lovable grandfather continued, "And you will go to sea. You don't think so now — but you will go."

By the time Chester reached his junior year in high school he had become more restless than ever. His grades were good and as he explored more areas of learning, it became evident that the Hill Country could not hold him much longer.

After Christmas a team of surveyors worked out of Kerrville and stayed at the hotel. Chester talked to the men and his restlessness increased. They told him he could sign on as an apprentice to carry the rod and chain until he learned how to use instruments. It was a way, they told him, to travel and continue his education.

The idea became more appealing as he thought about it. It likely would have taken top priority when he finished high school if the two young army lieutenants had not registered at the hotel.

It was the army that turned Chester Nimitz's life around completely — but not in the direction he had hoped it would go. As it developed, Grandfather Nimitz became a prophet in every sense of the word.

A unit from the Third Field Artillery from Fort Sam Houston, on the outskirts of San Antonio, had been assigned to train in the hills outside of Kerrville. Chester's new friends, the young lieutenants, were a part of this group.

In evaluating the officers Chester saw two young boys not much older than himself. He found out they had grown up in small towns located in remote areas similar to Kerrville. They had been given a college education without any cost to their parents. Now they could travel and see the world at government expense.

The smartly tailored uniforms appealed to Chester. The classic military boots and polished Sam Brown belts added to that appeal. Underneath the quiet exterior of the young boy from Tivy Mountain was a subdued romantic inclination to see faraway places with strange names he couldn't pronounce. The army and the uniforms were the starting point and he intended to make every effort possible to get there.

The two lieutenants, William H. Cruikshank and William T. Westervelt, who had just finished West Point, were encouraging but cautious as they talked to Chester.

"It will be difficult to pass the examinations to get into the Point," Westervelt told him. "To get in is one thing and to stay is another. They try to find out early what a man is made of. If you do get in, you will be mighty discouraged at times. Once you make it, though, you'll be happy you paid the price."

Chester was not discouraged. He had become accustomed to hard work and was not afraid of competition. He had fought his battles in the Texas Hill Country and was ready to continue fighting them on the drill fields in New York. The prospect of an army career all but engulfed him as he applied to Congressman James Slaydon of San Antonio for an opportunity to take the West Point examinations. He realized he was only fifteen years old and had another year in high school but he wanted to try it anyway. As he mailed the letter to the congressman he thought about what his grandfather had told him earlier in the year.

"There is no age limit on your future," *Opa* had said. "When you want something you can't start

At the Knee of Tivy Mountain 47

planning too soon. Be sure you know what you want is right for you and then go after it. In this country you grow up early — or you don't grow up at all."

Congressman Slaydon threw a roadblock in front of Chester's army career before it got started. He also discouraged any hope for an appointment in the future.

"There is no opening now," Slaydon told him, "and with so many career officers in the district whose sons get first priority, there is little likelihood one will ever come open for you."

Then before Chester could realize his hopes for a future in the army was gone, the congressman re-opened the door.

"I happen to have an opening in the United States Naval Academy," he said. "Are you interested?"

NIMITZ AS A MIDSHIPMAN.
— *Official U.S. Navy photo.*
Courtesy Admiral Nimitz State Historical Park

2

NIMITZ

The Midshipman

GRANDFATHER CHARLES NIMITZ and Chester taken when he returned after graduating from the Naval Academy.
— *Courtesy Admiral Nimitz State Historical Park*

4

Annapolis — Not West Point

The young man from Tivy Mountain received the news from Congressman Slaydon with mixed emotions. His dreams of a life in the army were shattered before they developed. On the other hand, the vacancy at the Naval Academy gave him a chance for a college education.

It also created another problem. Chester didn't know what to say. He had never heard of the Naval Academy. He didn't know where Annapolis was. For that matter he didn't know where Maryland was. The geography he had studied didn't include it.

In spite of all the unknowns the answer was clear. When he talked to the congressman he made his objectives known.

"I want a college education," he told him. "I don't know anything about the Naval Academy but if it will give me what I want, then I'm for it. Perhaps it will be the best after all. My Grandfather Nimitz will think so and he is important to me."

"The examinations won't be easy," Congressman Slaydon told him, "but I have an idea you will make it. I like the look in your eyes."

Chester's eyes were penetrating as he replied, "I intend to make it. Whatever it takes to get there, I intend to find it."

If Chester was fortunate enough to qualify for the appointment, it would mean missing his last year of high school. He would miss plane geometry and other important subjects that would have to be picked up on the outside. He could see it would be the most difficult challenge he could have.

The pride of the German-Texas community was never more in evidence than when it became known Chester Nimitz was studying to take the entrance examinations for the United States Naval Academy. Others in the community had never heard of the Academy either, but it sounded important just the same.

Helping Chester developed into a community project. The Hill Country people were determined that one of their own would succeed. Between January when he started studying and April when he took the state examinations his life was one that passed in review.

To prepare properly he began getting up at 3:30 a.m. and studied two hours, then stopped to do hotel chores. After breakfast he ran to school. He knew being in good physical condition was just as important as knowing the subject matter because the lieutenants had stressed the point.

Susan Moore, a longtime Kerrville teacher, instructed him in mathematics, geography, English, and history. John G. Toland, the Tivy High School principal, found time to help in mathematics.

Even his stepfather, Uncle Willie, found a use for his dormant engineering training. When the captain heard about this, he remarked sharply: "I'm glad the money I spent on that boy is finally paying off."

Uncle Willie had some doubts about Chester's ability to pass the examinations but he spent endless hours covering material that was certain to be included. There was no question about his help being vital.

By taking advantage of the help he received and combining it with his own ability, Chester passed the preliminary state examinations in April 1901. It was a red letter day for the people of the Hill Country. It was the first time anyone from the area had passed the examinations required to enter either of the service academies.

Captain Charles Nimitz had his grandson an admiral almost overnight. The proud old man arranged a celebration that was remembered by all who were to take part in it.

The first community *wurstfest* in Fredericksburg was held at the Steamboat Hotel in May 1901. Kegs of beer were brought from San Antonio for the occasion and people came from far and wide.

June and July passed quickly and as Chester prepared for his departure, the reality of it all began to close in on him. When he thought about leaving his mother, his Grandfather Nimitz, and the rest of the family, he realized what he would be giving up to reach the goal he had set for himself. There were friends he would miss as well as the familiar sights that he had come to appreciate, without realizing it. It had never occurred to him before but he suddenly realized he would miss being able to look out and see Tivy Mountain.

William Nimitz, whom he continued to think of as "Uncle Willie" rather than his stepfather, helped ease the situation. "You have dedicated yourself to climb a peak higher than Tivy Mountain," he said, "and you have just reached the first stop. There will be many more stops ahead of you that are worse and it will take a while to get there. You will be discouraged before you get to the top. But you will get to the top, of that I am sure. All at home will be waiting until you plant your flag at the highest point."

The congressman accompanied Chester to Annapolis in July after making the last stop at the Steamboat Hotel before the trip to San Antonio was made by stage. Grandfather Nimitz showed a lot of emotion when he told his grandson goodbye. The pride he enjoyed in seeing a dream come true reached out and covered other members of the family who might have been sad about Chester's trip that was certain to keep him away for a while.

The journey was to be a new experience for the fifteen-year-old German boy. It was his first trip to nearby San Antonio and he rode on the first train he had ever seen. Anna Nimitz had packed enough food to last the entire trip so they were well fed and comfortable. Chester looked out the window as long as it was light and then settled back and listened to the singing of the rails after darkness had set in. The congressman relaxed and went to sleep but Chester was too excited to do anything but close his eyes and think about what was ahead of him.

The Union Station in St. Louis bewildered Chester. He didn't know a building could be built that large. Congressman Slaydon saw the look on his friend's face. "What do you think about it, son?" he asked.

Chester just shook his head. "It's bigger than Tivy Mountain," he finally said.

His eyes were even bigger when they arrived in Washington. "The capital of the United States," he said to himself. "I never thought I would see it."

Chester had seen a map of Maryland which showed the Seven River and Chesapeake Bay but the real thing was breathtaking. The magnitude was beyond his reach and while he looked at the endless expanse of water he knew it was only an infinitesimal part of the water areas he hoped to become master of in the future.

The congressman was able to make things move a lot faster. Chester was immediately enrolled in the Werntz Preparatory School for further preparation. After concentrated study for just over a month, he took the competitive national examinations and passed with ease.

On September 7, 1901, forty years and three months before the attack on Pearl Harbor, Chester William Nimitz was sworn in at the United States Naval Academy as a cadet. He was beginning the switch from the Guadalupe River to Chesapeake Bay and a change from limited use of a small rowboat on the river to warships that would take him around the world. With the swearing-in ceremony he proudly declared his allegiance to America, the country that had accepted his ancestors from Germany and given them new hope and new opportunity.

Naval expansion at the turn of the century was responsible for Chester Nimitz's opportunity to break out of the confines of the Texas Hill Country. After years of neglect, members of Congress decided to provide funds for a new navy. The expansion began in the early 1880s and by 1898 the modern fleet had captured the imagination of the American people with a smashing victory over the Spanish at Manila Bay. Commodore George Dewey did a masterful job executing the victory and added a bit of romance to the action that appealed to young men who longed to go to sea.

Popular interest became more evident after the United States annexed Hawaii, the Philippines, Guam and Wake Islands, along with parts of Samoa. With President Theodore Roosevelt supporting naval expansion, Congress authorized the construction of at least one battleship a year between 1898 and 1921. The only year missed was 1901, the year Chester Nimitz entered the Naval Academy. That year shipyards were unable to keep up with production.

The United States Naval Academy was founded in 1845, the year before Fredericksburg, Texas, was chartered by German immigrants. It had a lackluster existence until the turn of the century. The class of 1901 with 131 cadets was the largest ever assembled, causing living quarters to be crowded. Chester had to live in temporary barracks part of the time. These were difficult to keep clean, besides being too hot in the summer and too cold in the winter. Because of his background, Cadet Nimitz fared better than some of his urban classmates.

With the expansion of the navy, members of Congress decided that the Academy needed a face lift. Many of the old buildings were renovated and front faced with brick. Construction of Bancroft Hall, the largest and most lavish dormitory ever built until that time, was started. Part of the building had been completed by the time Chester and his classmates began their final year and they were able briefly to live in style. Reports indicate that they made the most of their opportunity, even at the risk of being expelled from school.

Life was becoming dull for the group of the sophisticated First Classmen. They decided to liven it up with a beer party in the new wing of Bancroft and when the cards were cut to see who would get the refreshments, Chester "lost."

At the tailor shop in town where he was having a suitcase filled with beer he noticed a dark-haired gentleman in civilian clothes. The proprietor of the shop, who provided the beer as a special service to certain customers, didn't bother to introduce Chester, who was in uniform.

Monday when Cadet Nimitz reported to his navigation class he was shocked to see the stranger he had seen at the tailor shop sitting in the instructor's chair—this time in uniform. He was Lieutenant Commander Levi Calvin Bertolette, USN, class of 1887, who had just returned for a tour of duty at the Academy.

Nothing ever came of the incident. It is possible that Commander Bertolette did not recognize the cadet he had glanced at in the tailor shop but on the other hand he may have felt no harm was done and decided to overlook the incident.

The experience made a lasting impression on the Texas cadet. "It taught me to be lenient and look with tolerance on first offenders when they came before me," he said, something he was in position to practice frequently.

Through the years Chester hoped he would meet Bertolette in the service and thank him but their paths never crossed again.

"Boys will be boys," Grandfather Nimitz said when Chester wrote him about the incident. "I hope it was German beer."

Even with an expanded program to meet the increased demand for naval officers, the enrollment while Chester was in residence never exceeded seven hundred cadets. Strict class identification was maintained but there were no unknown students at the Academy. Because of his friendly attitude, Chester knew more cadets than most of his classmates.

After the bombing of Pearl Harbor, many of the critical decisions in the Pacific Theatre were more difficult because many of the officers involved were friends and classmates of the new Fleet Admiral, Chester Nimitz. Ernest King and William Pye, with whom he worked throughout the conflict, graduated in June before he was sworn in the following September. As a whole the class of 1905 stood out with an unusually large number of leaders.

Bill Halsey, the son of Commander William F. Halsey who headed the Department of Seamanship at the Academy, was a member of the class of 1904. He was a year ahead of Chester Nimitz in school but served under him throughout the Pacific War. Circumstances during their Academy years brought them closer than usual and created an understanding that lasted throughout their illustrious careers.

Among Chester Nimitz's fellow cadets were Harold Stark, Husband Kimmel, Royal E. Ingersall, John Towers, John S. McCain, Thomas C. Kinkaid, Fred Fletcher, Wilson Brown, Raymond A. Spruance, Milo Draemel, Aubrey Fitch, Robert Ghormley, Kent Hewitt, Kelly Turner, and Fairfax Leary, all of whom served well in the expanding navy.

Bill Halsey, nicknamed "Bull" by war correspondents, played two years on the Academy football team as fullback. "I was the worst fullback the Academy ever had," he stated frequently, "on the most inept teams in history. If they hadn't been so bad, I never could have made them."

Halsey and Nimitz became friends during the football season of 1902. Chester was too small for team sports except for crew but he enjoyed watching the games.

Halsey went by Chester's room late one Monday afternoon after practice. He was so mad it was difficult for him to talk. "I need your help," he told his friend.

It wasn't just Bill Halsey's problem. It involved all of the members of the football team who went directly to practice from a science laboratory in their coveralls. Coveralls were to be worn on special occasions and never as street clothes but for years football players had been ignoring the regulation and didn't bother to change before practice. They had been getting by with it because officers had been lenient and tolerated the exception. All had gone well until Lieutenant Lester A. Heiser was assigned to an Academy post in the summer of 1902.

Heiser — "Chicken Heiser" he was quickly nicknamed — was one who went by the book. It was soon evident that he made no exceptions. If the book said it should be done a certain way, that was the way he expected it done.

"Heiser gave four of us 'rams' today," Halsey explained. "We had on our coveralls as usual. That's three times for me and it means the Sunday 'Bull Ring' if I get caught again. I would have to walk off my demerits on Saturday if I wasn't playing football."

Chester believed in obeying the rules but he also realized that being practical was frequently the best solution. He didn't approve of Heiser's strict interpretation of street clothes.

"What do you want me to do?" Chester asked.

Halsey smiled. "You are the strategist," he replied.

Lieutenant Heiser, a bachelor in his early thirties, had only one interest and that was making progress in the navy. He had been frozen in rank on two tours of duty and it irritated him.

Wednesday was the only day he was not involved in cadet exercises and he often went to town in the afternoon. Usually he returned with an armload of packages which he carried up military walk to his bachelor quarters.

From the East Gate of the Academy where the public conveyances unloaded passengers, a military walk extended to the living quarters of the cadets and unmarried officers. A five-foot wire fence, in front of a solid privet hedge shielded the buildings set back from the street. Periodic openings with walks extending from the buildings were about twenty to thirty yards apart. A person coming from one of the buildings could not be observed until he stepped out on the walk.

The first Wednesday after Chester and Bill Halsey had talked, Lieutenant Heiser returned from town with a load of packages. As usual he started walking toward his quarters. At the first opening on military walk a cadet stepped out and brought himself to full attention with a salute.

Heiser was surprised but recovered quickly. He carefully laid down his packages, returned the salute, and packed up his purchases again. The same thing happened at the second opening. Then again at the third and at the fourth. By that time it had started to sprinkle and Heiser finally gave up. "At ease," he roared out as he came up to the fifth opening.

The following Wednesday Heiser returned without packages so his walk was uninterrupted. A week later when he again had his arms full, the cadets were there to draw his salutes. They were there every time he returned after that, packages or not. Finally the lieutenant put a stop to the procedure by dismissing them with a vocal command. It was also then that he stopped giving the football players demerits for wearing their coveralls to practice.

"The lieutenant could have still gone by the book and not returned the salute if he had his arms full," Chester told Bill Halsey, "but I was counting on him not taking the exception."

Bill Halsey grinned. "I told you I could count on your strategy to solve my problem."

Even though he had enrolled in the Naval Academy at the age of sixteen and had passed up his last year in school, Chester Nimitz still made good grades.

THE WILLIAM NIMITZ Family — Left to right are William, Otto, Dora, Chester, and the mother, Anna.

He followed the routine he had used in Kerrville by getting up at 4:30 a.m. and studying until reveille. His roommate, Albert Church of Idaho, did the same thing and they both received excellent reports.

They enjoyed each other and got along well. They discussed the different environments they had grown up under and the things they had done back home. Albert talked about hunting, which he enjoyed doing, and Chester told about the many fishing trips his grandfather had taken him on.

"We don't do much fishing where I come from," the Idaho boy said. "Up home we found it a lot easier to buy fish than to catch it."

Chester laughed. "We couldn't afford to buy it; but if we could have, I would have fished anyway."

Midway of the first semester, Chester received a setback when he became chilled and sick with pneumonia. He had to wait too long for his turn to use the bath facilities after becoming heated from an exercise class. The following month was spent in the hospital and he got behind in his studies. By the end of the year, however, he had caught up with Church again and it was then that the dean decided to separate them and give them new roommates who were in need of some extra help.

Chester Nimitz had never heard the word "hazing" until he arrived at the Academy, but it wasn't long until he was introduced to what was called "running" which was a form of verbal abuse. Physical contact was not allowed but the purpose of the procedure used was to eliminate those who lacked self-control when under extreme pressure.

"This is where we separate the men from the boys," the plebes were told but it didn't bother the sixteen-year-old boy from Texas. Perhaps it should have but Grandfather Nimitz had laid the background well. He took the mild hazing with little visual effect and finally the upperclassmen lost interest in trying to give him a hard time.

Chester continued to do well in his studies but he took every opportunity possible to learn things from outside the classroom. In later years he concluded that some of his most valuable experiences were not learned from the printed page.

Each summer the class was involved in maneuvers away from the Academy. In each case it involved

TWO ADMIRALS and a captain during their midshipmen days: (Left) Chester Nimitz, who became commander of the Pacific fleet one day before Royal E. Ingersall (far right) became commander of the Atlantic fleet. G. V. Stewart (center) served as best man in the Nimitz wedding.

— *Official U.S. Navy photo.*
Courtesy Captain Roy C. Smith III USNR (Ret.)

enlisted men from the regular navy. It seemed to Chester that at times some of the training officers tried subtly to show up the cadets as to how little they knew and how much they were expected to learn.

On one cruise a drill officer was performing in front of the cadets and used the sailors to stress his point. From the orders he gave, he had the enlisted men completely confused.

During an especially difficult drill, the instructor purposely reversed everyone in the company. Those who usually were on the right were on the left and those normally in the front were in the back.

He then asked if anyone could get them back in their proper places in just six orders. Several volunteers tried but failed. When he ran out of prospects he just stood there with a superior look on his face. Finally a cadet from Kentucky stepped forward.

With a pronounced accent he said, "I can get them back in place with just two orders."

The instructor didn't believe it. "Prove it, sailor," he said, with contempt in his voice.

The men were already standing at attention so the cadet gave his first order, "Fall out."

They did and he then gave his second order. "Fall in around me."

The men promptly fell into their proper places.

Because of the shortage of officers for the expanding navy, Chester Nimitz and his classmates were graduated on January 30, 1905. This was six months ahead of schedule and Chester was still less than twenty years old, one of the youngest midshipmen to achieve that status. With that rank they became "appointed officers" upon graduation, not commissioned officers. Eligibility to be commissioned with the rank of ensign came after serving satisfactorily in the navy for two years. Their service records were kept at the Academy and were available for review by the Academic Board.

Of the one hundred thirty-one cadets who enrolled in the Academy in 1901, one hundred fourteen graduated. In that group Midshipman Nimitz stood seventh in total achievement. His highest marks included mathematics and naval application — the practice cruise.

In fourth place was Royal E. Ingersall, who became commander-in-chief of the Atlantic Fleet the next day after Nimitz was assigned the same position in the Pacific area.

In the fifth class position was Fairfax Leary, who commanded several units in World War II which included the Allied naval forces in the southwest Pacific and the Eastern sea forces. All in all, sixteen members of the class of 1905 achieved the rank of admiral and none of them were "tombstone promotions" — a final advancement just before retirement.

After graduation, Chester Nimitz returned to Texas for the first time since he and Congressman Slaydon left in July 1901. It was a joyous occasion and to see the pride displayed on *Opa's* face made the entire experience worthwhile for Chester. While he was there one of the few pictures in existence today was taken with Chester and his grandfather together. Captain Nimitz's health was beginning to break and he found it increasingly difficult to move around. The return of his grandson, whom he had given to the sea, seemed to stimulate him and perhaps extended his life a few more years.

When his leave was over, Chester took a train from San Antonio to the West Coast. On the same train was Midshipman Bruce Canaga, a classmate of his, and they traveled to San Francisco together. Since they had identical orders, they reported for duty on the battleship, the U.S.S. *Ohio*. After serv-

USS *HARTFORD* — Fleet Admiral Nimitz served on this ship on his second class cruise while a midshipman at the U.S. Naval Academy in 1903.

— *Official U.S. Navy photo.*
Courtesy Admiral Nimitz State Historical Park

ing a short time together, they were separated but reunited on several subsequent occasions and remained friends for life.

As Chester Nimitz worked toward a permanent commission in the navy he frequently reflected on his life as it had transpired to date. Destiny, fate, or chance — with perhaps a little luck thrown in — seemed to be moving him in the direction he wanted to go. The strange turnaround from one service academy left questions to be answered but he ceased to think about it. The navy was now in his blood as Grandfather Nimitz had predicted it would be.

About the same time there was a similar force directing another Texas-born German boy. Although they never functioned in the same theatre of operation, they came together in the glory of victory on both sides of the world.

This young man wanted his education to come from a commission in the United States Naval Academy. Because of his age when he applied, he was turned down. Since the United States Military Academy at West Point accepted older appointees, he applied there and was accepted. Like Chester Nimitz he made the most of what had been offered him.

His name was Dwight D. Eisenhower.

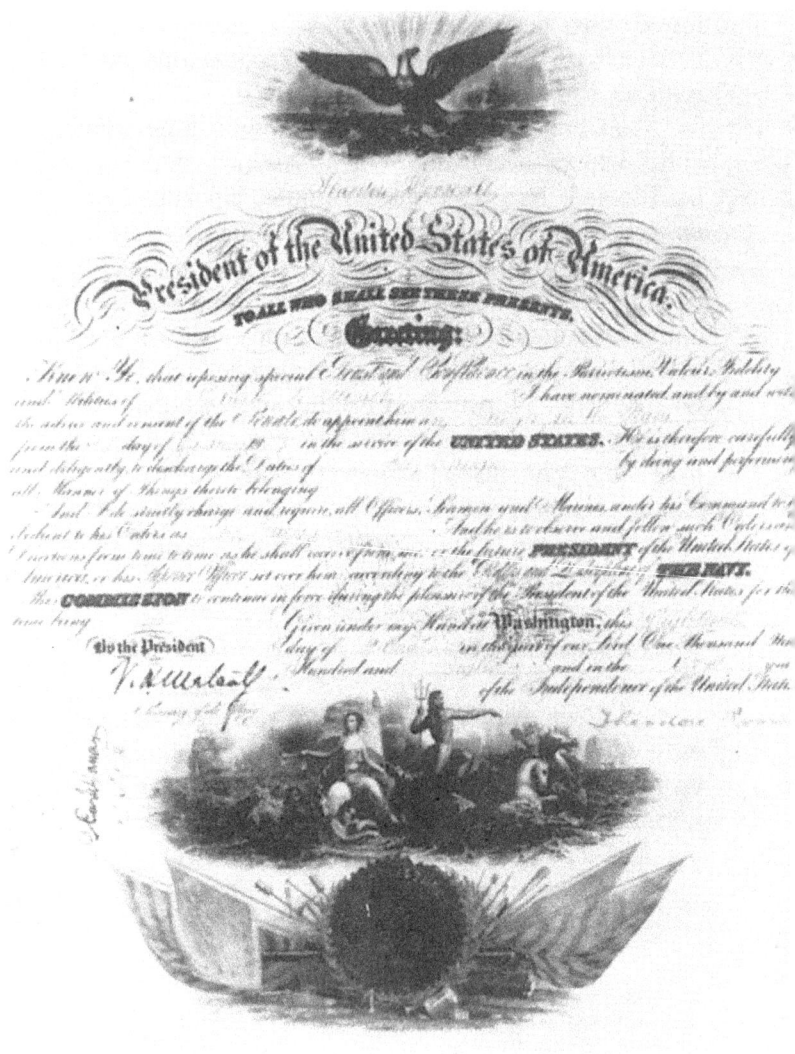

NIMITZ'S ENSIGN Commission received in June 1907.
— *Official U.S. Navy photo.*
Courtesy Admiral Nimitz State Historical Park

5

The Waves Rise Up

Chester Nimitz was a midshipman on the battleship *Ohio* before he was old enough to vote. Grandfather Nimitz had been right when he said, "In this country you grow up early — or you don't grow up at all."

The old innkeeper had been talking about the Texas Hill Country but Chester found the same was true in the navy. He also found out that age is relative, at least in his case. He was more mature than his years, a condition that helped as he gained responsibility. He found he could combine maturity with understanding to develop a strategy that would survive under the most difficult circumstances.

The *Ohio* was not the first battleship Midshipman Nimitz had served on. As a cadet in the Academy, he had summer cruises on the *Massachusetts* and the *Indiana,* both having seen service in the Spanish-American War. Even during the brief periods he was involved with these vessels that were considered the pride of the navy, he got the feel of the deck of a battleship and it never left him even though much of his time was spent in the submarine service or in command of the smaller cruisers and destroyers.

It was during a summer cruise that Cadet Nimitz acquired one of the minor physical ailments that became a part of his normal life. During this summer service on a cruiser he developed an ear infection and there was no doctor on board. The captain used a long-stemmed oil can from the engine room to squirt boric acid into the infected ear. The slight deafness that Chester developed may have been because of the abscess, or it could have been because another infection developed from the lack of sanitation while using the squirt can. During his active career he compensated by reading lips.

The *Ohio*, whose captain was Leavitt C. Logan, an officer with thirty-eight years of experience, was one of four battleships authorized by Congress in 1898. She had just finished her acceptance trials when Nimitz and Bruce Canaga came aboard.

It was while cruising on the *Ohio* that Midshipman Nimitz established contacts that were eventually to extend beyond his ultimate involvement in the Pacific. During his years at the Academy he had studied Japan as a potential enemy. The Pacific Ocean was carefully scrutinized as a possible theatre of war and the navy's fleet exercises were frequently designed with Japan as the opponent. These problems the students had to work out were far from games when they involved the Japanese. It was with some understanding then that Midshipman Nimitz made his first Japanese contacts while the *Ohio* was cruising in the Orient.

The war that Russia and Japan had been waging for several years reached a climax in 1905 when Admiral Heihachiro Togo destroyed most of the Russian Baltic fleet at the battle of Tsushima. Since he had sunk most of the Far Eastern armada earlier and the Japanese army had captured Port Arthur, the Czar of Russia sued for peace and agreed to mediation by President Theodore Roosevelt of the United States.

The *Ohio* was in Tokyo Bay when the Japanese emperor gave a garden party for the victorious officers of the army and the navy, along with honored guests. Since senior officers of the *Ohio* seemed uninterested in the invitations they received for the affair, six midshipmen, including Chester Nimitz, were sent to represent the ship.

The grounds of the imperial palace were covered with hundreds of tables and stocked with a supply of Russian champagne captured at Port Arthur. The festive occasion was in full swing when the midshipmen from the *Ohio* arrived late because of transportation problems and were seated at a table near the rear exit.

As the champagne flowed freely and the party began to wind down, the *Ohio* midshipmen saw Admiral Togo walking toward them as he prepared to leave. With the wine giving them courage, if not wisdom, the midshipmen decided to ask the Japanese leader to join them. It seemed logical that the midshipman from Texas should be the one to extend the invitation.

Togo smiled as he accepted, much to the surprise of the Americans. After shaking hands with all of them, he took a sip of champagne and then chatted briefly in English which he spoke fluently. Chester Nimitz never saw Admiral Togo again but the Japanese leader made a lasting impression on him. After becoming an admiral himself, Nimitz exerted considerable effort to preserve and honor Togo's memory.

The *Ohio* was the flagship of the United States

Asiatic Fleet and had a leadership role in guiding the rest of the fleet. A lot was expected of the crew and it was on the trip to the Orient that Captain Logan began to notice Midshipman Nimitz for his work as a boat officer. In his first report to the Academic Board at the Naval Academy Logan wrote: "I cheerfully recommend Midshipman Nimitz for consideration by the Academic Board. He is an excellent officer."

Because of the defeat of the Russian navy, the once cordial relationship between Japan and the United States became strained. This was due, in part to the type of peace treaty President Theodore Roosevelt, acting as mediator, had put together for the two nations to sign. The Treaty of Portsmouth was the document in question but the New Hampshire settlement was disappointing to the Japanese. It did not allow the indemnity they had requested to help build up their war-torn economy. Japanese leaders felt that Roosevelt had been partial to Russia because she was considered a western nation, as was the United States.

Under the circumstances President Roosevelt decided to call his capital ships out of the area. In mid-September when the *Ohio* started the return trip to her home port, Midshipmen Nimitz and Canaga were left behind. They had been transferred to the cruiser *Baltimore* which had been a part of Dewey's fleet in the battle of Manila Bay.

Although a naval career was important to Chester Nimitz, he remained basically, a family man and cherished the close ties he had developed while he was growing up. No matter where he was, he managed to write his mother, Grandfather Nimitz, and later his wife, Catherine. He wrote his grandfather more frequently than he did the others because there was a longstanding relationship there with a

The Waves Rise Up

magnetic appeal for letters. For Chester, letter writing seemed to be a quiet way of self-expression that allowed him to organize his thoughts and produced a private release for his feelings.

A letter written to Grandfather Nimitz from the Philippine Islands in December 1906, when he was still only twenty-one years old, showed the effort Chester was making to get a ship of his own. It also explained he was not worried about passing the examinations required to be commissioned.

"I told you about trying to get one of the gunboats down here," he wrote. "Well, the powers that be have assured me that I will have command of the U.S. gunboat *Panay* just as soon as she is ready to go into commission. She will go into service two weeks from now and will cruise in the southern islands of the Philippine group. Just look at a large map of this section and you will see what a big section it covers. These little boats get roving commissions — that is they can visit any port they choose. ... The crew will consist of about thirty men all told and I have been allowed to take my pick of the ship's company. ... I should have a bunch of good men."

The Texas Hill Country boy advanced in his naval career at a rapid pace. He and Bruce Canaga were commissioned ensigns January 31, 1907. In a short time Nimitz left the Philippines. He was given command of the *Panay* at Manila Bay and Canaga took over the *Paragua*. The two new ensigns spent much of their time cruising together without encountering any real problems. This period of roving duty was a time of excitement for both of them as they enjoyed not knowing what was beyond the next horizon or behind the next sunset.

Besides handling his gunboat, Nimitz was in charge of a small naval station, Polloc, a limited port on Mindanao. There were twenty-two marines stationed there and Chester spent part of his time on the island although he slept on the *Panay*.

"It was an exciting period," Chester later wrote home. "We had no radio, no mail, and no fresh food. We did a lot of hunting and some fishing."

When the men complained about having to eat so much duck, their commander quickly countered with an old German proverb: *"Hunger ist der beste Koch."* Hunger is the best cook. Then he related some of the experiences of his youth. "Why don't we try to catch some eel?" he asked. "My Grandfather Nimitz told me that eel and rattlesnake taste about the same. I have eaten rattlesnake and it tastes pretty good." The men suddenly became better satisfied with the duck they had been served.

It wasn't long after Chester Nimitz had taken over the little base at Polloc that Japanese activity changed his life again. A war scare involved the U.S. Asiatic Fleet and extended all the way to Mindanao. The attitude of the Japanese towards the United States was not clear as they were still upset over the Portsmouth Treaty not allowing the restitution they felt entitled to.

In evaluating the Russian defeat it appeared to have resulted from a strategy based on the "divide and conquer" theory. Togo and his commanders had first destroyed the Far Eastern Russian Fleet by catching it in small separate units. Then they waited for and destroyed the Baltic squadron as it arrived from the Atlantic. It therefore seemed logical that if Japan intended to move against the United States it would need to do so quickly before the Atlantic fleet could reach the Pacific. On such an assumption the Philippines seemed to be the probable place to begin an attack.

Nimitz and the *Panay* were summoned to

Cavite, the big naval base in the Philippines where he had been stationed while on the *Baltimore*. In his white dress uniform he reported to the base commander, Rear Admiral U. R. Harris, a sour-faced disciplinarian who seemed unable to smile. In his normal gruff manner he announced that Nimitz would take command of a destroyer, the *Decatur,* which was not in commission at the time. The job was to get her in drydock and hasten the preparation required to make her seaworthy.

Had the commander been endowed with a slight sense of humor, Chester might have smiled when he made the unusual announcement. Normally twenty-two-year-old ensigns were not given command of destroyers even during times of a pressing emergency. His contemporaries, Spruance, Halsey, and King, received their first destroyer commands between the ages of twenty-six and thirty-six.

Admiral Harris didn't allow Nimitz time to pick up his gear from the *Panay*. "Your clothes will catch up with you," he told him.

The *Decatur* was in poor shape when Chester Nimitz arrived in a launch greeted only by a Filipino watchman. After a thorough examination, he determined that much of the deterioration was reparable. In reality it was a good ship, having been commissioned in 1898 as part of the naval expansion program that produced the *Ohio* and two other battleships. It had been neglected through inactivity and needed a complete reworking which would require replacing many major parts.

At first Chester had a sinking feeling in the pit of his stomach when he thought of the job ahead of him. However, when he returned to the shore from the anchored ship and viewed the placid blue water of Manila Bay, he began to regain his optimism. Then when he looked at the wooded hills in the distance he became confident that he could show himself worthy of the confidence his superior officers had placed in him.

As often was the case, Chester Nimitz profited by his consistent practice of making friends without concern for rank or status. Several warrant officers, with whom he had played poker while the *Panay* was in drydock, were more than willing to do what they could to furnish the much-needed parts and supplies. By working day and night Chester and his bob-tailed crew were able to get the ship in top condition within the given two-weeks period.

It was well that the U.S. Fleet in the Pacific was brought up to a more respectable strength even if the war scare subsided almost as quickly as it had developed. The Japanese government expressed peaceful intentions by extending invitations for the Atlantic Fleet to visit Tokyo Bay when it reached the Pacific. This pleased President Roosevelt and he immediately made an unexpected counter proposal.

In a surprise move the president announced that the American fleet — The Great White Fleet, as it was called — would make a goodwill tour around the world that would include Japanese waters. It was a subtle way of reminding other countries of the strength of the U.S. Navy.

Making arrangements for the tour was Secretary of War William Howard Taft. After leaving Japan, he visited the Philippines where he had been a successful governor earlier from 1901 to 1904. He went to Manila in the fall of 1907 for a brief appearance at the opening of the General Assembly and then with Mrs. Taft and their young son, Charles, they visited other Philippine ports.

Ensign Nimitz became involved in the tour and was assigned to make the Taft party comfortable. He got an early start in this capacity by having a special chair made from two normal-size chairs to support the 300-pound future president.

There is no real evidence that Nimitz charmed Secretary Taft with some of his "tall Texas tales" but there is reason to believe that he did.

After he became president of the United States in 1909, Mr. Taft decided he wanted a place in the wide open spaces where the air was fresh and pure so he and his friends could relax at their leisure. Since most presidents normally return to their home states, the decision to have a vacation home in Texas instead of Ohio adds support to the Nimitz influence.

President Taft had a two-and-a-half-story frame house built near the little town of Catarina in southwest Texas. Catarina was a planned town that never completely developed and the Taft home stood unoccupied for many years after the owner left office. Only recently, in the spring of 1981, it was purchased by former Texas Governor Dolph Briscoe and moved to his large Catarina Ranch a few miles away. Here it will be a showplace for antiques the Briscoes enjoy collecting.

It was evident early that Chester Nimitz was a diplomat, if not a politician. He had the capacity to work with officials in office, regardless of political affiliation. As to his own preference, there is no solid evidence that he belonged to any party, especially during the first part of his navy career.

There is evidence that if Chester had been required to make a political declaration he would have been a Republican. The German community that took in much of the Hill Country had supported the Union cause during the Civil War and has voted for Republican candidates consistently since then. Grandfather Nimitz found out their preferences when he tried to raise volunteers for the Confederate cause when he was the captain of the Gillespie Rifles which replaced Federal troops that had been stationed at frontier forts to provide protection from the Indians.

Former President Lyndon Johnson had the political preference of the Hill Country made quite clear to him every time he ran for public office. As a Democrat he was never able to carry Gillespie County, even though his ranch home was in nearby Stonewall.

In spite of the diversified activity Chester Nimitz continued to be involved in, he was fast building up a desire to return to Texas and see his family. He had been away for three and a half years and he knew his grandfather's health was failing. Just how he would be able to make the visit was still unsettled but he intended to find a way if at all possible. The opportunity came sooner than he had hoped but through circumstances that certainly were not desirable.

Fate dealt a hand on July 7, 1908. Ensign Nimitz became a little careless in handling the *Decatur*. When he entered Batangas Harbor, south of Manila Bay, he estimated his position instead of taking bearings. He also failed to check to see if the tide was coming in or going out. Suddenly the leadsman called out: "We are not moving, sir."

It took only a few minutes for the grim realization to hit him that they had run aground on a mudbank. All attempts to move her off were without success and he faced a situation that could destroy his naval career. As his ship rested on the mudbank that dark summer night, Chester recalled what his grandfather had drilled into him as a youth. "Don't worry about things over which you have no control." With that recollection he relaxed and set up a cot on deck where he slept the rest of the night.

Soon after daybreak the next day the *Decatur* was pulled free by a small steamboat which happened to be passing by. This could have been the end of the story and no one would have known the difference but it was not in Chester Nimitz's makeup to try to get by with something that was dishonest or against regulations. He immediately reported the incident in detail.

Most of the officials who were involved in passing judgment on him would have just as soon had him to forget about it, but navy regulations required an investigation since it was reported. Ensign Nimitz was transferred to the cruiser *Denver* to await court-martial proceedings.

Because of his spotless record and the poor conditions of the charts for Batangas Harbor, he was tried on a reduced charge. He was found guilty of "neglect of duty" and received only a public reprimand. Except for the inconvenience and embarrassment, the court-martial brought Chester good luck. He had been relieved of the command of the *Decatur* so two weeks after the sentence he was on his way home.

For Chester Nimitz the trip home was a distinct pleasure. He sailed on the gunboat *Ranger*, a worthy craft that had been sent out as a training ship to be used in the Philippines. It was too expensive for the Filipinos to keep in operation so four Naval Academy graduates from the class of 1905 were assigned as watch officers to bring her back home. There she was assigned to the Massachusetts State Nautical School. Besides Chester Nimitz, the ensigns included Glenn Owen Carter, John H. Newton, and Alexander Wadsworth.

The *Ranger* reached Boston in early December 1908, exactly five months after the *Decatur* had been grounded in Batangas Harbor. Chester lost no time in catching a train to Texas.

The trip home was a rewarding one but there was also a note of sadness. Grandfather Nimitz's health was not good and Chester felt he might not see his beloved *Opa* again. For this reason he spent more time at the Steamboat Hotel than he might have otherwise.

Medical records during the early part of the century were frequently inaccurate and nearly always incomplete but Mrs. William J. Lawson of Austin, one of two living granddaughters of Captain Nimitz, feels that her *Opa* suffered from crippling arthritis. If this was the case, he fought it until the very end.

The old innkeeper used a rope device above the head of his bed to pull himself up by. Once he was up he could shuffle around his room and occasionally would get out in the hotel lobby. The visit from his favorite grandson seemed to give him new life and he lived two years and three months longer after Chester returned to duty. He died on April 26, 1911, at the age of eighty-five. The proud old man went willingly. He had experienced a full life and was well on the way toward realizing what he had set out to accomplish — to make a contribution to the sea by giving her an "Admiral of the Hills." Chester was unable to return for the funeral because of extended submarine duty.

After his trip to Texas, Ensign Nimitz received the disappointment of being assigned to submarine duty. Before he reported, he knew what to expect. While still at Annapolis he and his fellow cadets had taken turns studying the *Holland,* the navy's first commissioned submarine, which was anchored there for an indefinite period of time.

In those days, submarine service was considered hardship duty without extra compensation. For most navy men submarines were considered "odd looking contraptions which still had to be proven."

Chester continued receiving good news that helped offset the unpleasantness that came his way. Eighteen months after grounding the *Decatur* he was promoted from ensign to lieutenant having skipped the rank of lieutenant, junior grade. Grandfather Nimitz lived long enough to receive the message and with a smile that covered the tenseness brought on by pain, he proclaimed: "My boy is on his way."

And so he was. For a fifteen-year-old high school student who had progressed to a twenty-two-year-old navy ensign and had survived a court-martial without serious damage, Chester William Nimitz was "on his way."

USS *PLUNGER* (SS-2) renamed A-1, commissioned February 25, 1909. Admiral C. W. Nimitz was the third captain of this submarine.
— *Official U.S. Navy photo.*
Courtesy Admiral Nimitz State Historical Park

USS *PLUNGER* being renovated and renamed USS A-1.
— *Official U.S. Navy photo.*
Courtesy Admiral Nimitz State Historical Park

6

The Unexpected Charts A Course

For Chester Nimitz the unexpected always seemed to be just around the corner waiting to take over. This happened frequently and in a variety of forms.

One occasion was when his belated romance began to take shape. Under normal circumstances protocol would have directed him to pay courtship to the eldest daughter of a prominent New England family. Instead he became happily married to her younger sister.

Chester first met Catherine Freeman in November 1911 after he had returned from sea duty on the submarine *Narwhal*. Orders had sent him to Quincy, Massachusetts, to supervise the installation of diesel engines in the submarine *Skipjack*, anchored at the Fair River Shipbuilding Company. He was contacted by Lieutenant Prentice Bassett, a friend from his Naval Academy days, soon after his arrival.

Bassett, at the time, lived with his mother at

nearby Wollaston and invited Chester to join them for supper. Soon after they reached the Bassett home, Prentice suggested that they walk down the street and visit the Freeman family. Mr. Freeman was a successful ship broker but Chester soon found that the primary attraction was the Freeman's twenty-five-year-old daughter, Elizabeth. She was considered one of the most attractive girls in town and had more than her share of suitors.

Mr. Freeman invited the lieutenants to return after supper for an evening of bridge. To make any progress with Elizabeth, it was necessary to play bridge with her father.

The younger daughter, nineteen-year-old Catherine, wore the "little sister" label given her by Elizabeth who was very outgoing and sure of herself.

By comparison, Catherine was a retiring person and was inclined to stay in the background. Even so, Chester saw in her a stability and understanding that blended with his own way of thinking.

When the lieutenants returned for their bridge date, Elizabeth was away so Catherine took her place at the table. She became the partner of the young lieutenant from Texas, and a feeling began to develop between them almost at once that soon dispelled the old adage: "East is East and West is West, and never the twain shall meet."

Catherine began to feel naval officers were not such a bad group after all. Her evaluation of them had not been high because most of Elizabeth's friends were in uniform and they got in her way when her own company was there.

Another of Chester's acquaintances in Quincy overseeing the rebuilding of the submarine *Sturgeon* was Clarence Hinkamp. They had rooms at the one hotel in town and frequently ate together. The few restaurants, like the hotel, left a lot to be desired.

The Unexpected Charts A Course 85

Chester, who had been receiving invitations from the Freeman home for meals, managed on occasions to include his friend, who was called "Heine." Together they furnished humorous conversation for the ladies and provided father Robert with bridge partners. As time passed Chester and Heine managed to spend more time with the girls at the expense of the bridge game. Chester and Catherine were always together while Heine and Elizabeth made up the foursome.

When the *Skipjack* and the *Sturgeon* were ready for their trial runs, the two officers who were constant visitors at the Freeman home, continued their close association by taking the submarines out together. They cruised as far south as Chesapeake Bay before returning to their home port.

Chester managed to write Catherine a letter every day even though some of them were short. One in March was unusually brief. "I had to go swimming yesterday and it was awfully, awfully cold."

In a letter to the Freemans a few days later, Heine explained what had happened. A sailor on the *Skipjack* had fallen overboard and when Chester saw he was a poor swimmer, he jumped in to help him. It was a struggle against the man, as well as the current, and Chester found it difficult to keep from being carried out to sea. Fortunately they were sighted by a lookout from the battleship *North Dakota* and were picked up.

For a navy lieutenant to endanger his life to help an enlisted man impressed sailors and officers alike. It showed early in his career that Chester Nimitz took care of his men.

Heine assured the Freemans that there had been no complications and Chester was in good health. For his heroic effort, the Treasury Department awarded him the Silver Lifesaving Medal.

USS *NARWHAL* — Nimitz was commanding officer from November 18, 1910, to November 23, 1911.
— *Official U.S. Navy photo.*
Courtesy Admiral Nimitz State Historical Park

USS *RIGEL* — Nimitz was the commanding officer from June 17, 1931 to September 30, 1933.
— *Official U.S. Navy photo.*
Courtesy Admiral Nimitz State Historical Park

The Unexpected Charts A Course   87

It was an award the Texan always wore proudly. He considered it one of his choice awards. He confided in Catherine years later that he appreciated it because it was earned for saving a life, not for helping take one. He made it clear that he disliked armed combat, but as a navy man his assignment was to help protect his country which at times required action that would take lives.

In the summer of 1912 the romance of Chester and Catherine reached a point of no return as far as "big sister" was concerned. Elizabeth had continued to supervise Catherine, even in the presence of company. By then Catherine was nearly twenty-one and resented being treated like a child.

The submarines were based at Provincetown Harbor on Cape Cod, near where Prentice Bassett, who by then had married, had a cottage. Frequently the three couples got together on weekends and enjoyed many activities with one another.

One day they were having lunch on Prentice's ship and wine was being served. Elizabeth, whose table was across the room from Chester and Catherine, got up and walked over to her sister. "You mustn't drink any wine," she said in a positive manner.

Her voice carried throughout the room and Catherine was embarrassed. She turned away as Chester took over. He looked Elizabeth in the eyes and spoke in a calm but positive tone: "Elizabeth, I am looking after your sister. I have no intention of letting her drink too much wine but she will have a glass if she wants it."

As a result, Catherine's attitude changed toward her entire family. She knew her only requirement in the future would be to please the young officer whom she was counting on to be her partner for life.

On August 28, 1912, only a few days after the

wine incident, Chester wrote his mother in Kerrville, Texas.

"My dear Mother:

If you love me at all, I want you to congratulate me on becoming engaged to Catherine B. Freeman of Wollaston, Massachusetts, to be married in April or May of 1913, just after I leave the submarines and before I start my tour of shore duty."

The letter was long and filled with detail but Chester let it be known he knew what he was doing and had made up his mind. He explained his financial position to his mother and indicated that his half brother Otto, who was also a graduate of the Naval Academy, had met the Freemans. Otto would fill her in with more of the details on his next leave which would be coming shortly.

The wedding took place at the Freeman home on April 9, 1913. Chester, as commander of the Atlantic submarine flotilla, had spent the previous winter in Cuban waters. Originally he had planned to return to Kerrville during the Christmas holidays. From the time he was a little boy at the Steamboat Hotel in Fredericksburg and his Grandfather Nimitz had told the story of *tannenbaum* and Kris Kringle, Christmas had been a time he enjoyed with his family.

During the cruise in Cuban waters Chester had been in command of the *Skipjack* and Clarence (Heine) Hinkamp continued as skipper of the *Sturgeon*. Most of the planning for the wedding was done by mail during that time so all was taken care of when he arrived the day before the ceremony.

The Freemans had the wedding in their home and it included a large number of friends. Because of the uncertainty of an exact date, Chester's relatives from Texas were not able to attend. He had written his mother to expect him and Catherine to visit her before he returned to active duty.

Elizabeth Freeman was the maid of honor and Lieutenant George Stewart, one of Chester's roommates at Annapolis, was the best man. The ushers were submarine officers with one exception. Catherine's older brother had come back from Michigan where he was studying mining engineering.

The expression, "Always a bridesmaid but never a bride," seemed to fit Elizabeth Freeman. She never married, although she was considered attractive and was blessed with an outgoing personality.

Some of the New England neighbors didn't know what to say to the handsome young lieutenant from Texas. Although they admired his white dress uniform, to them he lived in a world that didn't exist.

He was asked: "Do you ever see Indians?" or "Do you have friends that are cowboys?" One lady smiled and said: "Lieutenant, I hear you are from out west."

Chester replied, "Yes, m'am. I'm from Texas."

The lady smiled again and said, "I've been out west."

Chester quickly asked: "Where out west? It's a big place."

"Cleveland," she told him.

After the reception the newlyweds took a train for New York. Catherine had been out of Massachusetts only one time, so it was quite an experience for her. The size of the city surprised her, but they occupied the time window shopping, walking in Central Park, and seeing the landmarks. They saw a couple of shows but saved their money since they still had the Texas trip to pay for. At the time Chester's salary was only $215 per month. From this amount, he sent his mother $25 every payday.

The Texas trip almost proved to be a calamity.

If the New England guests had been curious, many of the Texas Germans were suspicious and resentful. They weren't ready to accept that "Yankee girl" who had taken their Chester.

There were exceptions, of course. Anna Nimitz responded graciously to her new daughter-in-law. And William, because of his college years in Massachusetts, related to her easily. Grandmother Henke, who was almost seventy, made the trip from Fredericksburg to Kerrville to see her new granddaughter-in-law. She was genuinely responsive in a manner that made Catherine like her immediately.

"I have never been treated with more courtesy than I was by Chester's mother and grandmother," she wrote her parents in Wollaston.

Even if the Nimitz and Henke relatives were not inclined to welcome the new member of the family with open arms, they recognized her as a gifted and talented person who had dedicated her life to being a good partner for Chester. Before the visit was over, they had warmed up to Catherine and she began to feel welcome.

"Our people are reserved," Anna Nimitz told Catherine. "We are slow to warm up to strangers, but you have been accepted now and have their support."

Chester and Catherine returned to Washington and were pleased to find orders for him to study diesel engine construction in Germany. Lieutenant Nimitz was considered the foremost expert on diesel engines in the navy, but his knowledge of the larger motors in this country was limited. Arrangements had been made through the German government for him to study at the Blohm and Voss Shipbuilding Company in Hamburg, Germany.

The newlyweds sailed in May, 1913, about a month after their marriage. While in Hamburg Chester worked hard, and they made a trip to Nürnberg to visit another diesel plant. Finally, they were able to get in a quick visit to Denmark and southern Sweden before leaving for the United States.

When they returned home at the end of the summer, Catherine was pregnant. They took an apartment in Brooklyn where Chester had been assigned to the machinery division of the nearby New York Navy Yard. They then settled down to plan for the arrival of their first child.

Catherine Vance was born in Brooklyn on February 22, 1914. She had missed her father's birthday by two days.

With the arrival of the little girl who was named after her mother, Chester and Catherine began being the typical all-American family. Chester was a devoted father who tried to be strict but frequently didn't manage it.

He had a manner of handling the children, however, that commanded their respect and gained their love which meant so much to him.

Brooklyn was an American melting pot that threw fathers of all professions together in the park with their children while their wives were preparing Sunday dinner. Chester, without his uniform, was one of the boys.

Chester Nimitz, Jr., who was also born in Brooklyn, came along on February 17, 1915, and was his father's son from the beginning. As he grew older he picked up the nickname "Calamity Joe" for an accumulation of an unusual number of ailments, ranging from a cracked head from falling off a building, to a badly burned ankle caused by an exposed wire. He might have been considered as accident prone, but Chester, Jr. had every right to say: "Hey, wait a minute — I think I inherited some of that."

He could have at that. Things seemed to continue to happen to Chester, Sr. with about the same degree of regularity. It began with a slight deafness developed during his student days and continued throughout his life. While in Brooklyn he was knocked unconscious and covered with a pile of lumber from a platform built around the *Maumee,* a 14,500-ton oil tanker he had been working on. There were no bones broken but he was sore for several days and the back trouble he suffered years later likely originated from this experience.

Soon after the platform collapse, Chester experienced an accident that came close to ending his navy career. His sister, Dora, related her version just before she died.

"My older brother and I were very close. I always called Chester my brother, never my half brother. But he teased me and called me his three-quarters sister.

"The first time he came home after graduation, I admired his class ring and he told me I could wear it. Of course it was way too large, but I wrapped string around it and wore it anyway.

"Then when I saw him after he married, he told me he missed his ring and hated to ask me but he would like to wear it again. I knew how he felt and even though I sure hated to give it up, I took it off right then and gave it back.

"Chester was showing a group of people how the new diesel engines worked, while he was stationed in Brooklyn. To protect his hands from the grease he wore cotton gloves which had fingers about an inch longer than his hand. In pointing to a set of cogs he wasn't noticing how close to them he was and the glove on his left hand got caught in the wheels. It was his class ring that stopped the cogs and let him pull his hand out. Of course, he lost part of his finger. But had it not been for his ring he like-

CLASS RING from the Naval Academy that likely saved Chester Nimitz's hand and also his navy career.
— *Courtesy Admiral Nimitz State Historical Park*

ly would have lost his entire hand which would have ended his navy career."

Besides the series of accidents there were organic disorders that seemed to come at inopportune times. However, in some cases the changes caused by the illnesses were to his liking.

After Chester had recovered from his latest accident and had almost completed work on the oil tanker, the *Maumee,* he had the opportunity to leave the navy but was emphatic in his decision to remain. At the time his navy pay was $240 per month with a subsistence allowance of an additional $48 a month.

Lieutenant Nimitz was still considered the top diesel engineer in the navy and his talents did not go unnoticed. The Busch-Sulzer Brothers Diesel Engine Company in St. Louis offered him $25,000 a year to come with them and guaranteed a five-year contract. According to an associate sitting near him, Nimitz thought about it only briefly and then said: "Thank you, but I do not want to leave the navy."

The *Maumee* was being sent to the Gulf of Mexico to refuel ships there and Chester had been assigned to inspect the work he had done. Catherine decided to take the children to Texas, since Chester would be in the area.

At the second meeting, Catherine could not say enough about the courtesy of her mother-in-law. "She made me feel so welcome," she reported. "She is a handsome woman with a lovely laugh and a demanding smile."

The *Maumee* refueled at Port Arthur on the Texas coast and Anna Nimitz was only too glad to keep the children while Catherine and Chester had a brief visit. Back home, Catherine shook her head and smiled: "I didn't have to spank the Grandmother Nimitz out of the children, but it got close at times."

After the Texas trip on the *Maumee*, Chester was promoted to lieutenant commander and transferred from the tanker service to an engineering aide for Captain Samuel S. Robison, commander of the submarine force, Atlantic Fleet. It may have been the most important change in his career. In Captain Robison he found an excellent leader, a strong supporter, and a lasting friend. By being assigned to Captain Robison, he was able to change his professional direction from machinery to people. He seemed to be on the verge of finding a new vocation.

The Nimitz family moved to Washington and on

September 13, 1919, Catherine gave birth to another daughter. They named her Anna after her maternal grandmother but the resemblance ended there. Active and inquisitive, little Anna was everything her namesake was not. The name Anna didn't fit and she became known as Nancy, to which she has answered since then.

Before being assigned to duty with Captain Robison, Chester Nimitz spent the time during World War I in the Mediterranean and part of the Atlantic. Germany had broken her word on the use of submarines and it was necessary to combat her efforts against merchant shipping.

Things quieted down at the end of the war in 1918 and Chester got a breathing spell. He was able to spend more time with his family. But in 1920 it started all over again.

In June he was ordered to build a submarine base at Pearl Harbor using World War I salvage. As was usually the case, his assignments were demanding and carried high odds against success.

With a map of Pearl Harbor and the help of four chief petty officers who had developed a lasting loyalty to him, the thirty-five-year-old lieutenant commander completed the job on schedule and earned new recognition.

When the base was ready, Chester Nimitz was promoted to commander and assigned to remain as commanding officer at the Hawaiian base. As he sat in his new offices little did he suspect that he would return in twenty years as the commander-in-chief of the Pacific Fleet.

The movement of the Nimitz family during the next ten years included much navy activity, but included more time as a husband and father.

A shot in the arm for Chester came in 1922 when he received orders to attend the War College, an assignment he had been hoping for. It would allow the opportunity to obtain a position in the high command. He knew the time was right for such a move. He wondered about the timing. Perhaps it came because of a recommendation by Captain Robison or it could have been helped by his work at Pearl Harbor.

After moving from Honolulu to Newport, Chester was sent back to the West Coast to organize a Navy R.O.T.C. unit at the University of California at Berkeley. He was in every sense of the word regular navy but he also favored a program in which civilians could have limited participation. As usual, he did an excellent job.

The years spent as a teacher and faculty member at the University of California were some of the most rewarding he experienced. The prospect of having a forty-one-year-old navy officer with only a provisional college degree as a department head with the status of a dean was upsetting to many of the members of the faculty who rather enjoyed basking in their pomposity. In time, however, it worked itself out.

The Navy R.O.T.C. program was a new experience for those in the school at Berkeley, as it was in other colleges that were involved. Acceptance for the young naval officer came after he explained the purpose of his work and how it would give added strength to the U.S. defensive posture. He was popular with the students from the beginning and broad-minded staff members soon joined them. He learned from his faculty associates and in turn he was able to add to their own storehouse of knowledge. The fact that the Naval Academy did not grant a normal academic degree was offset by his rank as an officer. This designated experience in excess of the time required to earn a Ph.D. degree. The Nimitz family made some lasting friendships at Berkeley and it was with reluctance that Chester moved on to the next assignment in his rapidly accelerating career.

The West Coast appealed to Chester and Catherine and they decided to settle there after their moving days were over. Chester had become commander of Submarine Division 20 based at San Diego when he received a letter from William P. Fairlong, a classmate at the Academy. It dealt with a twenty-fifth year anniversary yearbook, which Fairlong was editing, that was being put together to show the history of the class of 1905.

The reply covering the progress of the Nimitz family was brief but complete, with one exception.

"I have enjoyed every one of my assignments and I believe it has been so because of my making a point of becoming as deeply immersed and interested in each activity as I could possible become," he wrote.

He went on to say: "My life in the navy has been a very happy one and I know of no other profession for which I would have forsaken my present one."

He concluded with an account of his family. "My oldest child, Catherine Vance, age 16, is about ready for college and my boy, Chester William, Jr., age 15, hopes to enter the Naval Academy in the spring of 1931. My third and last child is a daughter, Anna Elizabeth, age 10. My wife, my children, my profession as a naval officer, and my good health combine to make me a happy man."

As he wrote the letter, Commander Nimitz seemed to have forgotten the unexpected that was waiting around the corner. It showed up again on January 17, 1931, and they named her Mary Manson Nimitz. This time she was the last child of this typically all-American family.

Mary's arrival came at a time when her father was undergoing a change in duty. He became commander of more than thirty of the decommissioned

USS *TALBOT* — While commanding the *Plunger* Nimitz twice commanded the *Talbot* for special operations on July 6 and July 16, 1909.

— *Official U.S. Navy photo.*
Courtesy Admiral Nimitz State Historical Park

destroyers from the San Diego base. This was when the Nimitz family moved from their apartment to the *Rigel*, a tender moored near the inactive destroyers.

This assignment, perhaps the most unpleasant of his career, came to an end in the summer of 1933 when he was ordered to take command of the new heavy cruiser, the *Augusta*, and report with her to Shanghai where she would become the flagship of the Asiatic fleet.

The purpose of the Asiatic fleet was to patrol the China coast in a public relations type of performance, visiting ports, and performing according to international protocol. Mrs. Nimitz and the girls were able to join the commander but Chet was enrolled in the Naval Academy.

In June 1934 the *Augusta* paid a visit to Japan at the time Fleet Admiral Togo was at the point of death. This Japanese hero had defeated the Russian fleet at Tsushima in 1905. Nimitz recalled meeting the admiral on his first visit to Japan and how impressed he had been with the humility of the man.

A company of the most impressive sailors and marines available — all over six feet tall — were sent from the *Augusta* to march in the procession. Flags were flown at half-mast and a nineteen-gun salute was fired in honor of the admiral. The next day, Nimitz and Admiral Upton, who had accompanied him from China, attended the simple funeral at the modest home of Togo, located in a wooded area outside of Tokyo.

In 1935, Captain Chester Nimitz was sent to Washington as assistant to the Chief of the Bureau of Navigation, a desk job he was not happy with but accepted with good grace as a part of his naval portfolio. Here he was united with his old friend, Captain Bruce Canaga, who had made the long train trip with him from San Antonio to California where they began their navy careers on the battleship *Ohio*. They shared a car pool that served the Navy Department and enjoyed recalling their experiences while walking the last mile or two to the office.

In Washington, Chester Nimitz had a chance to practice the time honored Texas tradition which was based on the philosophy that "stolen fruit is the sweetest fruit." He had felt it imperative to follow regulations and report the grounding incident of his ship, but he would pick all of the cherries he could reach through the fences along the street where he walked.

On one occasion, a lady caught him and a friend enjoying her reachable cherries. Chester listened patiently as she scolded them and when she had finished, he complimented her on the quality of the fruit, the beauty of her yard, and the attractiveness of her home. Her belligerence wilted under his charm and she invited them to return for more cherries.

While in Washington Chester and Catherine were able to attend the graduation of Chester, Jr., who, after a short leave, went to sea aboard the cruiser *Indianapolis*.

Events then began to accelerate for the Nimitz family. In the spring Chester was elevated to the rank of rear admiral and was delighted to learn he would be going to sea once again. Orders came in May that he would report in early July to San Diego to take command of Cruiser Division Two.

Mrs. Nimitz had agreed to christen the new submarine *Sargo* at Groton. Then on June 18 Chet was to be married in the chapel at Mare Island Navy Yard, near San Francisco. To keep all the dates from conflicting took careful planning.

After they had given the newlyweds their blessings, Chester and Catherine hurried to San Diego where he took command of his flagship *Trenton* on

NIMITZ RELIEVES Rear Admiral J. O. Richardson as Chief of the Bureau of Navigation in June 1939. He is being sworn in by Rear Admiral W. B. Woodson.

— *Official U.S. Navy photo.*
Courtesy Admiral Nimitz State Historical Park

July 9, 1938. At that time he met Lieutenant Preston Mercer, his new flag secretary. Nimitz was commissioned as an interim rear admiral on July 30, retroactive to June 23.

Once again the unexpected took over. The Texas admiral developed a hernia that needed immediate surgery. The month in the hospital, along with additional time for recovery, cost him what he thought at the time was an excellent opportunity.

Fortunately, for Chester, this was not the case. He lost the cruiser command but after his recovery he received orders to take over the more desirable Battleship Division One command.

In early January 1939 most of the U.S. Navy was involved in conducting Fleet Problem XX in the Caribbean area. Admiral Nimitz was left as senior naval officer on the West Coast, commanding Task Force Seven which consisted of his flagship, the *Arizona*, a large cruiser, several destroyers, auxiliary vessels, and a tanker. The basic objective for this group was to develop a procedure for underway refueling, and practice amphibious landings.

The assignment was pleasing to Nimitz. He had already concluded that there would eventually be armed conflict between the United States and Japan. He felt the experience he had gained while commanding Task Force Seven would be used. He was determined to have the American forces perform better than the enemy.

The program was making excellent progress when it suddenly hit a roadblock. Nimitz received orders in early 1939 to return to Washington and serve as Chief of the Bureau of Navigation in the Navy Department.

The unexpected had taken over once again and for Chester Nimitz this was not the end of the line. It appeared again on December 7, 1941.

3

NIMITZ

The Man

FLEET ADMIRAL Chester W. Nimitz shown with part of his finger missing from the accident where his class ring saved the rest of his hand.
— *Courtesy Admiral Nimitz State Historical Park*

7

The Portrait of a Leader

The bombing of Pearl Harbor sent shock waves throughout the world. Each person then alive remembers where he or she was on that date, December 7, 1941. They vividly remember how they received the unbelievable news that the Japanese had attacked the United States Fleet at Pearl Harbor.

Chester Nimitz described exactly where he was on that date as it became forged in his mind like a rivet in a steel plate. It was a Sunday early in December and the day was crisp and bright. The sun penetrated through clouds on that icy afternoon helping to warm the hearts and hearths of families settling down to nap. Chester and Catherine Nimitz lounged lazily in the living room of their apartment in Washington, D.C., listening on their radio to Arthur Rodzinski conduct the New York Philharmonic Orchestra.

Bombs and Beethoven do not mix. The mood was quickly broken when an excited radio commentator interrupted the symphony to bring the staggering message — Pearl Harbor, our naval base in Hawaii, had been attacked by the Japanese.

Nimitz bolted from his seat. He had to go to the office even though he didn't know how badly the unexpected attack had damaged the fleet. He grabbed his cap and topcoat as the telephone rang. Captain John F. Shafroth was calling to say he would pick the admiral up immediately and take him to the Navy Department. Nimitz put the phone down and asked Catherine to call his aide and flag secretary, Lieutenant (jg) H. Arthur Lamar, and tell him to join him at the office. With this he kissed her goodbye as he made a single sobering statement, "I won't be back until God knows when."

The time it took for Nimitz to travel by car from his home to the Navy Department seemed endless. Each block became a mile and each moment a month.

When he arrived, Nimitz learned the grim truth — much of the United States Pacific Fleet was sunk in the mud of Pearl Harbor. Hangars and buildings were burned. Two hundred planes were destroyed right where they stood and thousands of sailors, soldiers, and marines had been killed or injured. The shock was beyond belief, the emergency crucial.

Nimitz also learned that Admiral Stark, the Chief of Naval Operations, with the consent of President Roosevelt, had radioed the U.S. Navy's first combat directive to all commanders in Panama and the Pacific area: "Execute unrestricted air and submarine warfare against Japan."

The United States was at war!

The next few days were a scurry of activity and confusion. More retired and reserve personnel were ordered back to duty. Information was wrapped in a cloak of security. The expansion underway because of the war in Europe went to full speed. Many orders were sent out and the already busy days in Washington became feverish and hectic.

The Nimitz household was also turned upside down. In a space of hours a relaxed Nimitz, who lived comfortably with his family and followed a fixed routine, was catapulted into a new era of moment-by-moment decision making. Uncertainty lived with all of them and each knew that life would never be the same again. They were now a part of a fast-moving picture that had taken on a kaleidoscope of change, and they knew it.

Chester Nimitz knew it most of all. The normally taciturn Texan began to weigh his situation privately. His overall aggressive nature and his sense of fairness came into play. He had never liked war, but if it came, he wanted to play a vital role. His academic preparation and training was in wartime strategy. For the past two years he had been involved with navy personnel but his previous training prevailed. The sea was his mistress. Nimitz knew the dangers of the sea as well as the uncertainties of war. Strategies and plans had to be matched with the action of the enemy. He knew that in doing so authority must be absolute. At sea authority was as vital as food. It had to be absolutely unquestioned. The sea held its own law and that law was administered by strong and courageous men who knew when to bring about quick and immediate action. Nimitz felt the surge of the sea within himself. He heard the call of the bosun's pipe. He caught the current of war and was ready. One way or another Nimitz was preparing in his mind to go to war.

In two days Secretary of Navy Frank Knox left for a personal inspection of Pearl Harbor. The next ten days all hands were on deck at the Navy Department. Calls and emergency duties swamped all the offices. When Knox returned to Washington, he re-

ADMIRAL NIMITZ being sworn in as chief of Naval Operations in 1944, relieving Admiral King.
— *Official U.S. Navy photo.*
Courtesy Admiral Nimitz State Historical Park

ported immediately to President Roosevelt. The next morning, December 16, the navy secretary called Nimitz on the phone before they met later in the day.

The conversation Knox had with the president was brief and to the point. "Tell Nimitz, to get the hell out to Pearl Harbor and stay there till the war is won," Roosevelt had shouted.

Nimitz was stunned. Why? There were twenty-eight admirals with senior rank to him. Two years ago he had declined to be considered when his friend, Admiral Kimmel, was chosen to go to Pearl Harbor. Instead, he stayed in Washington as Chief of the Bureau of Navigation. Now Nimitz was assigned without precedent and to add to his own hesitancy he was taking a command away from a longtime friend. Under normal circumstances this would not have set well with him, but Kimmel was in trouble. In the navy, duty was without compromise and Nimitz was a navy man. On December 17, 1941, Chester W. Nimitz accepted the appointment of commander-in-chief in the Pacific and went to war as a four-star admiral.

History does not list the twenty-eight senior officers Nimitz passed over but the *Navy Register* of 1941 lists them in alphabetical order. Nimitz knew their names, their talents, their abilities, and their style of leadership. Nimitz thought about the president's selection. He had to ask himself why had he been chosen over such a cadre of experience and rank?

To answer that question it was necessary to get inside the minds of President Roosevelt and Secretary of Navy Knox. One would have to know the qualities of leadership they were looking for and the type of man needed.

In retrospect, it can easily be said the president and secretary made a wise choice, but this is judging after the fact. To make such a judgment in the heat of battle was another matter.

Actually, Nimitz had expressed his own personal doubts to Secretary Knox. The Pacific command should go to Vice Admiral William S. Pye, who had been commander of the battle forces ad interim after Kimmel was relieved of duty. This was a natural reaction for Nimitz since he knew Pye was in line for the job. He also knew that had the situation been different at the time of the Japanese attack and he had been in command, the same thing could have happened to him. Nimitz was realistic and he was also practical.

What was it about this soft-spoken, determined man that set the minds of desperate leaders to choose him above others in line? What, in the Nimitz record, indicated he was the man for this monumental task — this unprecedented situation? Perhaps, it was a strange combination of characteristics both acquired and natural that composed his makeup.

No historical document could ever reveal the process used in making the decision but there were certain qualities that stood out boldly about this man and his career. Chester Nimitz had the qualities of greatness in his character. He was a family man who loved his home and his friends. Most of all he loved his country. He always spoke with pride of his son and his three daughters. He cherished his academic associations and he maintained a sense of value as well as a sense of humor that always simmered just beneath the surface of his smile.

On the other hand there was little in Nimitz's record to suggest that he should be the one picked by a president to provide the strategy of a new war. He had had a couple of years of battleship and cruiser duty and he had commanded Submarine Division 14 and later the submarine base at Pearl Harbor. He had a year at the Naval War College at the senior level. These were routine duties of an officer and could have been considered plush appointments. Only the early period of 1926-29 can be said to have offered true combat preparation. After that, he organized a Reserve Officers Training Corps at the University of California, a highly successful pioneer effort.

His capacity for making friends stood him in good stead throughout his career. This often underrated quality, though neither showy nor dramatic, provided a backdrop for his success. In making friends he learned about people. He studied men in every area of association. He learned about their strengths, their weaknesses, and their talent for leadership. He took pride in seeing that the officers under him were given assignments for which they were aptly suited. This ability, alone, served the navy and the country long before Pearl Harbor. It improved the effectiveness and the efficiency of day-to-day operations and would now enhance his new role as commander-in-chief of the Pacific.

That those above him knew or considered all this is speculation. What they knew was that Nimitz got along. In his low-key approach to life he maintained a second place posture while doing a first class job. He didn't seek publicity from the press nor popularity from naval personnel. He simply did the job his way — and his way proved surprisingly successful.

Nimitz's love for sports and classical music helped him to achieve a balance not only of interests but of character. History at this period of unparalleled crisis needed a man with a controlled balance to produce confidence, motivation, and follow through. He was not a devotee of opera — much of it was too heavy for him — but he did appreciate and listen every Sunday to the symphony. It was a time he set apart as one might a religious service and he was faithful to it.

Believing that care cured carelessness and patience had no substitute even in the time of war, Nimitz set forth to prove these two traits before the eyes of skeptical men. They wanted a rough, fireball, no-nonsense man.

Bill Ewing, an officer on Nimitz's staff and later editor of the Honolulu *Star-Bulletin*, said when he first saw Nimitz standing on the second deck of the administration building in Pearl Harbor he looked more like a retired banker than the kind of hell-for-leather leader needed to pull us out of the worst hole the country had ever been in. Nimitz's white hair and his fatherly expression belied the inner strength that set his flint-like face toward victory. His eyes could sparkle under the power of a pun or pop with anger and resolution when a hard decision had to be made. Pearl Harbor's crisis seemed to strain patience and caution with the country now at war. The United States had to prepare to defend itself in the face of the stupendous odds brought upon it by one fiery-hellish Sunday.

To his credit Nimitz maintained a delicate sense of balance under adverse circumstances. If the air in the map room became too tense Nimitz would get up a game of tennis or suggest a long walk to let everyone cool their heels. These exercises he found succeeded in not only cooling their temper but keeping them physically in shape.

When our forces received heavy casualties Nimitz's face would reflect the agony of failure and his determination for revenge. He knew that many more would die before the war could end but he never ceased to feel personally responsible for each life he ordered into battle. The responsibility weighed like an anchor around his neck.

The Portrait of a Leader 113

As the war deepened to the South Pacific and the fleet seemed hopelessly inadequate, Nimitz overcame the temptation to "damn the torpedoes" and order full speed ahead. For instance, there was the uncertainty as to whether the marines should stay on Tarawa where over 3,000 casualties had been reported in the first few hours of fighting, or to continue to attack. To stay meant more lives would be sacrificed. To withdraw meant even more men would die. The difficult decision was made — the marines stayed.

Later at a press conference General Howland "Howling Mad" Smith, who was the acting commander of the marines at the time, said the marines's willingness to die accounted for the victory — but it was more. From that moment, the commanders of the war in the Pacific lunged forward and never looked back.

This sense of controlled balance, poised between wanting to be active and needing to buy time, no doubt, came as a result of Nimitz's constant participation in sports. A relatively short man, five feet nine and a half inches, and not tipping the scales at a heavy figure prevented him from playing football. Consequently he took to lesser known activities of his time and while in Annapolis he had a starting slot on the rowing team. This gave him a sense of timing and established him as a team man. Due to Nimitz's small stature, the coach assigned him the stroke oar in the fourth crew. By setting the pace, the fourth crew began to win over the third crew and before long Nimitz progressed to the third. The third soon overtook the second and ultimately the second over the first. Nimitz found himself the stroke of the first crew where he paced seven men, each of whom outweighed him considerably. This overcoming characteristic became a pattern of behavior he relived over and over again.

At fifty-seven when Chester Nimitz was assigned to the Pacific fleet, he was advanced over older men with more experience. In time these men looked to him for leadership. He valued their contributions and respected their judgments. Nimitz knew how to unite the skills and abilities, not only of his staff, but of all the Allied forces combined.

There were times when conflicting personalities clashed and strong views of his staff members were pitted against one another. This, coupled with the frustration of short supplies and poor communication, caused tempers to flare. Nimitz held the line. After allowing the discussion to continue until the heads were as hot as the room temperature, he would frequently come up with a joke that broke the spell, defused the anger, and brought a ripple of laughter among the men.

Nimitz's contagious and refreshing sense of humor prevailed throughout the trying days of war. On almost any occasion he would come up with an anecdote. Friends throughout the country knew his fondness for stories and sent them to him. He used them regardless of how good they were if they were clean, fun-loving stories. Rarely did he tell an off-color joke even in the intimacy of his closest comrades.

Some of his jokes were excellent, some were simple puns and bad puns at that; but the laughter, his as well as the listeners, relaxed him. He knew that laughter was the key to a healthy and happy crew.

Nimitz also used puns to enliven the spirits of the men at sea. Making a pun about the Midway battle, he announced to the returning men, "We are now midway through the war."

When the admiral wasn't relieving mental and physical stress with a game of horseshoes, bowling, or handball he was enjoying his hobbies of collecting mottos or experimenting with gardening. Nimitz utilized mottos to their very best advantage — especially the one sent him by Admiral Halsey. It read, "The Lord gave us two ends; one to think with and one to sit on. The war depends on which we choose — heads we win, tails we lose." Above Nimitz's outer door to his office were these words: "Nations, like men, should grasp time by the forelock instead of the fetlock." One of his favorite he attributed to Theodore Roosevelt, "If you need a hand, try the one on the end of your arm."

He also put his interest in gardening to work both around his office and at home by taking hollowed out coconut shells and filling them with moss. In these quaint "pots" orchids were grown. He also supervised his own vegetable garden. This interest in the early years of the war prompted him to bring to Hawaii the dean of the College of Agriculture of the University of California who supervised the planting of plots big enough to provide fresh vegetables for the people in the hospitals.

The natives observed these interests of Nimitz and applied his ideas to their needs for better living habits. These were evidences of an unusually dependable man, but there were other characteristics, underlying his entire behavior pattern that helped to distinguish him from all other men.

First, he had unquestionable energy. His long hikes and daily walks plus his insatiable enthusiasm for sports recharged him for consistency and good health. Even the act of firing a pistol served to revigorate him for the difficult moments that came during the war years.

Nimitz slept little. From the time he was a boy he had more important things to do than sleep. He maintained the practice of going to sleep around ten or eleven and sleeping until three a.m. He would then get up, read or study, and then around five o'clock take a catnap for about an hour. This adequately prepared him for the day. Rarely, if ever did he take naps in the active part of his life. He didn't need to. The high level of energy sustained him and supplied him with the coping mechanism to deal with major life situations.

Nimitz took moderate to high risks and this played an important role in his overall analysis. Never one to turn the duty over to anyone else or blame another for what might be his own responsibility, he was able to take risks needed for victory in his own life or in the life of his country. He considered himself responsible for his own decisions and never was one to back away from making one. When there were alternatives, he would seek them out; but when spur of the moment decisions had to be made, and often they did, Nimitz did not falter. He had the confidence that his decisions were better than most others due to his past experience and his specialized training. He knew the rules of strategy and he knew how to play the game.

To say that war was like a game to Nimitz is to place the gravity of war in too light a framework. It certainly was not that, but Nimitz liked games. He enjoyed the finesse that went into winning both from the practical and the theoretical points of view. He played cribbage whenever he could. The nuances and subtleties of the game relaxed him and it kept his mind agile. To Nimitz play was re-creation. It allowed him to step out of the rigidly defined and limited role of a professional naval officer. Though there was never a conscious attempt to make what he did a game one could see the correlation between his ability to play and his move to turn all activities into a plan for winning.

This sense of play could also be found in the type of music he enjoyed. Instead of opera he chose a symphony, which may have been an indication of the depth to which he appreciated and understood harmony. As the war progressed and the forces enlarged the need for harmony among the services was acute. Nimitz felt all along there should be some unifying conductor whose task it was to blend the best of all forces into one, making the whole stronger than any of the separate parts.

Like in music, Nimitz was not a solo lover. He didn't appreciate the prima donna on the stage, in business, or on the battlefield. He didn't appreciate being upstaged by a younger officer, but he would never require undue attention to be brought to himself over a statement he made or an appointment he gave. He felt his job was to orchestrate the naval forces with all Allied forces in order to produce harmonious results.

Nimitz was very conservative. He was born and raised in the Southwest in the German custom and convention of a male-dominated society. He never outlived its values. He revered women as women, not as male substitutes, wearing pants and doing a man's job. It was difficult for him to associate with women in line of duty. He considered them special and looked at his wife and three daughters in a very loving way, always a part of him, but never as a threat to him. Outside of the navy Nimitz had no political ambitions. Ambition, to him, did not necessarily mean an advancement for self as much as what the self could do. Performance was the criteria of excellence, not personality. He could make a speech when called upon but was never considered a speech maker or a statesman. He didn't prophesy or predict, he merely tended to the job at hand and felt that was enough for one man, if that man did the job to the best of his ability.

The portrait of Nimitz is drawn in direct contrast to MacArthur. His low profile, while not appealing to the press, served him well throughout the war. Their taste for recognition was diametrically opposite. Nimitz bore a certain amount of dignified humility that General MacArthur never exhibited or appreciated. And to MacArthur's frustrations, Nimitz was wise enough to recognize that his own humility acted as an adaptive function for him in times of high level meetings, extreme intense situations, and in potentially embarrassing circumstances. The simple act of walking when he could ride in a chauffeured car or writing a memo himself rather than dictating it provided a human element to what he did and therefore communicated to his peers and his admirers. He traded on his humility as MacArthur traded on his arrogance.

Nimitz traded on his sense of humor in a different way. He used it at every point for effect and results. Consequently he was one of the most likeable men in the service regardless of rank or station. Lacking in flamboyancy did not hurt him. Rather, he gathered up respect like a father gathering in his children and even the apprentice seamen could sense one didn't have to cut through a facade to reach the true man.

Quietly and unassumingly Nimitz won the respect of his men. He may not have been what they thought they wanted — a rough, tough commander — but he brought to the job a sensible, workable approach that was both sensitive and stable. He wore well. His quiet personal drive brought forward the best of himself and others. As a strategist he planned with meticulous precision and as a tactician executed with authority.

In time he became the man with the quiet power who weathered Wake Island, Midway, and the Philippines, all with style and dignity — all the way to victory.

THE OKLAHOMA capsized with the *Maryland* in the background, Pearl Harbor.
— *Official U.S. Navy photo.*

4

NIMITZ

The Admiral

SOME CREW members evacuate during Pearl Harbor attack.
— *Official U.S. Navy photo.*
Courtesy Admiral Nimitz State Historical Park

8

To Sea By Train

Nimitz looked at the telephone and thought how strange it was that such a mechanical device could change the lives of so many people. The dilemma bothered him only momentarily since he couldn't allow himself the luxury of idle contemplation. Time was of the essence and he had to get started.

The telephone call had informed Nimitz of his appointment as commander-in-chief of the Pacific and that his new assignment was Pearl Harbor. He was shaken by the news and knew the release would hit the streets and be aired on the radio by nightfall. Catherine should be the first to know and he wanted to be the one to tell her.

Secretary of the Navy Frank Knox told Nimitz in the telephone call of another immediate assignment: Captain Randall Jacobs, Nimitz's assistant, was to replace him as Chief of the Bureau of Navigation — later called Bureau of Personnel.

Nimitz realized the urgency of the message. Ten days had passed since the bombing of Pearl Harbor and Knox gave him only seven days to get there. Jacobs' whereabouts concerned him. He would have to take over his new responsibility without Nimitz's assistance. As it happened, Nimitz would take over at Pearl Harbor without an initiation period.

Captain Jacobs rushed back to Washington after being away on an assignment. Running up the steps of the Navy Department building, he literally ran into the new commander-in-chief of the Pacific.

Nimitz grabbed Jacobs and asked if he had heard the news. Realizing Jacobs knew of the assignments, Nimitz said, "The job is yours, Randall. You know more about the bureau than any other senior officer. Come on, we'll go up and write your orders."

Chester Nimitz later walked home because it was the quickest way. As he moved along he planned his speech to Catherine. It didn't help the situation any when he found her in bed suffering from a head cold.

As he sat down beside her, he showed in his face concern for her health. "It's a bad time to tell you of my new assignment. I have been appointed the commander-in-chief of the Pacific and must leave as soon as possible. I hope you understand."

"All navy wives understand, Chester. They may not like it but they understand. My pride in you makes it a little easier. You have always wanted to command the Pacific fleet. Now your dream has come true and no greater honor could be given you."

"But, my dear, the fleet is at the bottom of the ocean. I have to build a new one from scratch—and we are at war. Each dawn will bring a new tomorrow for a long, long time."

"Just remember what your grandfather always told you—you'll make it." She smiled and patted his hand.

The German boy from Texas remembered — as he had the night he grounded the *Decatur* on a mudbank. He especially remembered the part about not worrying. It was at times like this his thoughts went back to his childhood and he subconsciously longed for the comfort old *Opa* might give him. As he thought, Nimitz recognized the melody playing on the radio. It was the new song, *Deep in the Heart of Texas.*

Opa was with him.

The next two days involved closed meetings and conferences with Admiral King, Secretary Knox, and President Roosevelt. Then on Friday, December 19, his flag lieutenant, Hal Lamar, again arrived, this time to escort the new fleet commander to California.

It was agreed that secrecy was necessary and the trip should be made incognito. Nimitz and Lamar would wear civilian clothes and use assumed names. Nimitz chose Freeman, his wife's maiden name. Lamar used Wainwright as his alias. The two were soon aboard a crowded train as Mr. Freeman and Mr. Wainwright.

On the way to the station the men stopped by the Navy Department for last minute instructions. Admiral King and Secretary Knox were there with Admiral Stark, the Chief of Naval Operations, and the Nimitz staff. It was a somber and formal goodbye, similar to his farewells with the family. Duty demanded protocol and no one was more conscious of this than naval personnel.

The staff members shook hands with Nimitz in a fond and genuine farewell. King spoke of his admiration and wished him the greatest success in the world. Then Stark handed Lamar a heavy canvas bag with specific instructions: "Don't let this bag out of your sight. When you are clear of the Chicago station, then and only then, turn it over to Admiral Nimitz."

The situation before Nimitz was staggering. He realized that many lives were dependent upon his

126 ADMIRAL OF THE HILLS

A JAPANESE ATTACK carrier from which the "Kate" torpedo planes took off as the crew cheered on December 7, 1941.
Official U.S. Navy photo

To Sea By Train

making the right decisions. For the first time he began to feel the fear of living in doubt and danger. His life would be covered by a blanket of secrecy and communication would be limited and guarded. This brutal war must be mastered for victory to be attained. The success of his command depended largely upon his decision as to whom he should tell what, when, and how much. He became silent as he left the department. The strain was beginning to move in on him.

Lieutenant (j.g.) Lamar had been cautioned by his superiors to look for such symptoms of strain and his order was to do all possible to keep Nimitz mentally and physically in shape during the trip.

The secret papers had to be withheld for the first few hours of the journey to assure this. Much assessment was needed by the man in the dark blue suit who was setting out on an engagement unlike any other that had ever developed. He needed time and the proper frame of mind.

Mr. Freeman and Mr. Wainwright boarded the B&O Capital Limited calmly and without incident and found their bedrooms. The canvas bag appeared an unnatural attachment to any business man but the two were fortunate to be supplied with a made-to-order camouflage. A swarm of college students crowded the train terminal eager to get home for the holidays. So no eyes were on Nimitz, even though the morning newspapers had spread all over the front pages President Roosevelt's first decisions since the Pacific disaster. The president apprised the American public that a five-man board, headed by Supreme Court Justice Owen J. Roberts, would investigate the disaster at Pearl Harbor. Further in the news was the appointment of Admiral Nimitz to replace Admiral Kimmel in the Pacific area. Admiral Pye would act until the arrival of the new commander. Nimitz was the man to watch — but fortunately, no one was paying any attention to him on the train.

Actually, Nimitz wanted no publicity as he had never been one to seek the limelight. He needed time to be alone, to think and absorb the magnitude of his mission. The overwhelming responsibility was beginning to weigh on him like a granite boulder from Tivy Mountain. All the prior planning for combat in the South Pacific had been "shot to hell" now that the Japanese had made the first move.

The Fleet Admiral needed rest. The past ten days had been a steady stream of on-the-spot decisions, each one building up internal pressures that filled his total being. Nimitz, conscious enough of his own needs, had made the suggestion to travel by train rather than by air. Isolated from the pressure cooker of the Navy Department, he could more nearly assess his situation and contemplate his future.

Nimitz knew he had to do three things immediately. He had to establish his own style of leadership, put it into practice as quickly as possible, and make no apologies. He had to learn all he could about the present strategy, not from reports or communiques, but from on-sight observation; and above all he must rebuild the American Pacific fleet second to none.

Privately, Nimitz reviewed his past in order to establish his future. He remembered as a young midshipman being dubbed "that man of cheerful yesterdays and confident tomorrows." Sitting in his bedroom he called up that confidence he sorely needed.

Always Nimitz had been a man who grew with his job. His style of command was one of patience and persistence. During World War I when he was operating under the command of Admiral Robison, he began to develop his theories of leadership. From the beginning he felt that leadership consisted of picking good men and helping them to do their best. The attributes of loyalty, discipline, and devotion to duty on the part of subordinates must be matched by patience, tolerance, and understanding by superiors. "Loyalty up and loyalty down," the navy called it and Nimitz began to mold that concept into his own manner of operations.

One of the basic qualities that enabled Nimitz to grow with his job was his intuitive ability to predict well in advance events of importance that would help shape his future and the future of the country.

A typical example of this ability was pointed out by Chester, Jr., who graduated in the class of 1936 at the Naval Academy, when he spoke at the commissioning of the USS *Nimitz*.

He said as a midshipman on leave at home in Washington after graduation he asked his father what his career plans were — was he really working for top command? The senior Nimitz replied that yes, he did have aspirations for top command, but thought the way to achieve it was by a demonstrated first-class performance in whatever job he was given.

After briefly shifting the pencils on his desk, he continued. He stressed the fact that when war came, and he was sure it would come, he hoped he would be in a senior command ashore. When Chester, Jr. asked why ashore, he continued.

"It is my belief that we will likely be caught flatfooted when war does come, the commanders at sea will be relieved, and I would hope to be one of the reliefs instead of the relieved."

As the new CinCPacFlt Nimitz reviewed his options. Would the real war be between the army and the navy in the South Pacific or would it be between the present staff and the new command? He had the feeling, as he thought of MacArthur, that the real war might well be waged in the conference room among strong-minded men — between two men in particular, himself and MacArthur. This was more than a projection for Nimitz. It was a fact he knew he would eventually see and must learn to live with.

Nimitz suddenly realized how deeply absorbed he was in his thoughts. He needed to balance this with exercise, even on the train. He called Lamar from the next room to supply some needed companionship. One might say it was time for a few stories.

Lamar was stunned at the sudden change in Nimitz's manner. He had left a sober man to his thoughts and returned to one with a twinkle in his eyes.

This was the first time Lamar had heard the tall tales from the man from Texas. Some of them even dealt with his own experiences. Nimitz started teasingly: "The first time I did armchair duty in Washington I learned a good short cut," he said. "Haven't ever used it myself. I'm not put together that way but a lot of people have.

"There was a big room full of ensigns not long out of the Academy. In fact, a few of them could have done with a little more time there. Anyway, this one ensign over in the corner was having a time with his paper work. His desk stayed stacked. He worked nights and weekends, but it didn't help much.

"Across the room was another young ensign from Brooklyn. Somehow he managed to keep up without much of a problem. His desk was clear every morning by ten o'clock. After that he visited or talked on the telephone.

"Finally, the ensign with the stacked desk cornered him. 'I want to know something,' he told him.

'How do you keep your desk so clear? I can't do it.'

" 'It's simple,' the Brooklyn ensign told him, 'When I get a directive, I write 'Refer to Ensign Smith' and put it in the out basket. In all this mob there is bound to be an Ensign Smith.'

"The other ensign responded with a pained look on his face. 'Hell, no wonder. I'm Ensign Smith.' "

It was a tossup as to who enjoyed the session more—the man who told the stories or the man who laughed at what was said. Either way it made the trip go faster and much more enjoyable. It also set the scene for a good night's sleep—one long awaited by Nimitz.

The next morning the train pulled into Chicago and the transfer was made on schedule to Santa Fe's Super Chief. The admiral and his aide felt for the first time that they were on their way west.

After lunch, Lamar handed the canvas bag to Nimitz and then excused himself. He left the admiral to an afternoon of study of the secret papers.

Nimitz was shocked as he opened the bag and read the official report of the casualties at Pearl Harbor and saw the pictures of the sunken and damaged ships. As he carefully studied the pictures his spirits fell almost as low as the ships that had been sunk. One of the most heartrending pictures was the one of the *Arizona*, encompassed with smoke and her foremast leaning as if broken at the elbow. The report read: "Over a thousand of her crew — dead!"

Nimitz sat with the photo in his lap for a long time. It had been only three years since he was commander of Battleship Division One. The *Arizona* had been his flagship. His good friend, Captain Isaac Kidd, had succeeded him as commander and had acquired the same flagship. Nimitz was certain Rear Admiral Kidd was on board that fateful morning. The loss was both a personal and professional one and his emotions surfaced in private grief over the tragedy.

As Nimitz continued to study the report more and more he came to believe that the tragedy was not the fault of Kimmel. Until the investigation uncovered more of the hidden story, he preferred to leave it that way. Sick at heart as he was, he knew there could be no one more distraught than Kimmel. The guilt must be devastating. At the flag level the navy did not tolerate failure. Kimmel was human and Nimitz felt for him — but for the grace of God, thought Nimitz, there go I. He inwardly knew that the tragedy could have happened to anyone — it could have happened to him.

Nimitz pondered the problem. The fate that is dealt to others is a story within itself — and Pearl Harbor was destined to be a part of his life story as well.

To relieve the monotony and the constant clacking of the train wheels Nimitz slept when he could. Cramped quarters prevented his physical fitness program. All he could do was play cribbage with Lamar, read, and walk the narrow aisles. Occasionally he would go out on the station platforms when the train stopped long enough. In time he began to unwind and soon he started what was the first of a long series of letters to Catherine, filled with love and hope for the future.

Writing Catherine became his escape valve. He could tell her the doubts and fears that invaded his thinking. He could share with her his frustrations and confusions and open up to her his ideas for operations yet untested. He could tell her his gripes because she had always been his sounding board. She stood on the distaff side of all emergencies. The very act of writing Catherine relaxed him and served as a spur that enabled him to balance his moods.

As the Super Chief snaked across the open prairie in the westward trip to California, he continued his letter, "As I get more sleep and rest, I find myself less depressed about the situation. Things are looking up and I am sure by the time I reach Pearl Harbor I will be able to meet the requirements of the situation. I only hope I can fulfill the expectations you and Mr. Roosevelt have in me. It is an awesome task and I need your prayers."

After he had finished his letter, he called out to Lamar another Texas proverb that had occurred to him, "Lamar, always stand for something or you will fall for anything."

Late on December 22, the two men arrived in Los Angeles. Here they parted. Lamar returned to Washington and Nimitz proceeded on to San Diego.

In San Diego, his scheduled departure was delayed by abominable weather. Too much was at stake to take a risk. The Coronado was not the heaviest plane in the air and the flight was too risky. During the layover the admiral received the first of many radio dispatches:

ADMIRAL ERNEST J. KING, APPOINTED CHIEF OF NAVAL OPERATION

When the winds and rains subsided the next day, Nimitz boarded the plane and was off for the overnight flight to Pearl Harbor.

As dawn came up, the navy flying ship, appropriately painted black, began its descent into Hawaii. Chester Nimitz realized he was arriving on Christmas Day. He looked down below at the bomb-gutted debris and he knew it wasn't a good time or a proper place to sing "Joy to the World."

He congratulated the crew on a pleasant flight despite his lack of sleep and his anticipation of taking over his new command. He apologized for taking them away from their families and friends on Christmas Day, an attitude these men were not accustomed to.

As the plane landed smoothly in the harbor close to Ford Island after breaking through the early morning fog, Chester W. Nimitz, the Texas-born admiral, began to hum — "O Come All Ye Faithful."

9

Fleeting Up

At seven o'clock on December 25, Nimitz left the Coronado, and was met by a solemn reception committee. Admirals Kimmel and Pye were the first to come forward and greet their new commander. Rear Admiral Patrick Bellinger, commander of the Naval Air Unit in Hawaii, and Captains William Smith and Harold C. Train, chiefs of staff to Admirals Kimmel and Pye, waited in the background. To them the new commander extended his hand as he said, "My name is Nimitz".

Still in his civilian clothes, Nimitz bore no resemblance to an admiral of the United States Navy. He was rumpled and weary from his trip but his mind was clear and anxious for the first news of the war. "What do we hear from Wake?" With this Pye handed him the latest radio dispatch:

ENEMY ON ISLAND
ISSUE IN DOUBT
WE ARE STILL HERE
MERRY CHRISTMAS

NIMITZ DRESSED for action.
— *Courtesy Admiral Nimitz State Historical Park*

In trying to maintain a welcoming attitude, the men had no other choice but to update the report for their new commander. Wake had surrendered!

Silently Nimitz and his entourage drove to his new quarters at Makalapa. The house had been occupied by Admiral Kimmel until the last few days. Kimmel had quietly moved in with the Pyes until they both received new orders.

The new admiral quickly changed from his heavy winter suit to cooler khakis. It was evident the new uniform had not been fitted to him as it was becomingly oversized. No doubt, it was the first time Nimitz had ever worn a khaki uniform.

Nimitz then invited Admiral Pye to be his guest for breakfast as the terrible sights of devastation had openly affected him. He was not prepared to remain alone. As they ate, Kimmel joined them. He was wearing only two stars on his uniform—a demotion from his four-star rating prior to the Japanese attack. Again Nimitz's sympathy surfaced as he looked at the broken man. Kimmel's confidence appeared to be shattered. He had been forced to stand by helplessly and watch his fleet destroyed.

Though Nimitz couldn't see the bandage on Kimmel's chest, a report indicated he had suffered a slight flesh wound. The spiritual wound he suffered was deeper than any bullet could penetrate. He had told Pye earlier, "Too bad it didn't kill me."

Nimitz took him by the hand, "My friend, it could have happened to any of us. Stay here and help me. I need you more now than anyone else."

There are two things a new admiral does that make his command official: he hoists his flag and organizes his staff. As a new four-star admiral, Chester Nimitz required a flag with four white stars on a blue background. So on December 31, 1941, he hoisted his own flag at the submarine base in South-east Lock, Pearl Harbor, on the submarine *Grayling*. He then called a staff meeting.

Those attending the Nimitz meeting knew admirals had their own preferences as to the staff personnel. Each man summoned had served under Kimmel and Pye and had spent years "fleeting up" or being promoted within one's own fleet. Their morale was at the lowest since the news of the fall of Wake Island. As they entered the conference each staff member was resigned to the fact that Nimitz would want his own men to follow him at Pearl Harbor. Each man therefore came prepared for his transfer orders.

To the utter amazement of the entire staff, Nimitz began the meeting in an informal way. He told them he had suggested, even insisted to the president, that Admiral Pye be named the new commander-in-chief of the Pacific but had been overruled. He then made his first dramatic move toward rebuilding the esprit de corps of his new command. He expressed his faith in each man for his ability. Then he asked them all, as he had with Kimmel, to stay aboard. This simple expression of confidence began the first restoration of self-respect. He persuaded them that he could not adequately serve without their help. He also helped their morale by adding that nobody held them responsible for the most humiliating disaster in the nation's history. He believed all Americans were guilty of falsely assuming that no enemy would ever invade the United States or any of its possessed lands. This had now happened and people all over the world were stunned to hear the unbelievable news.

Nimitz was determined that these men, along with the navy, would not be further disgraced. He intended to be sure no one would be court-martialed.

The transformation of the attitude and spirit of

THE MAP ROOM for guidance.
— *Official U.S. Navy photo.*
Courtesy Admiral Nimitz State Historical Park

these men was like a curtain being raised on a new play. Their loyalty, as well as respect, shifted to their new chief.

This rare quality of Nimitz illustrated his ability to unite people and weld them into a team for concerted action. Normally he would have taken the first three months of any new assignment to build his own team. This was the style of leadership for the navy and particularly with admirals, but he did not have time for such luxury. He therefore decided to make changes only when changes were necessary. At the moment he had to use the men available. To revitalize their worth and credibility was a bonus they would never forget and created a loyalty that was never lost.

As soon as Nimitz had finished his staff meeting they went into the map room. For the first time the admiral of the Pacific looked over his territory from a new perspective. Every American naval ship that sailed those uncertain waters was now under his command.

The vast expanse of restless ocean was outlined on a string of maps thumbtacked to the wall behind the admiral's tabletop desk. With Pearl Harbor as a starting point, the area stretched out some 5,500 miles to Panama and up to the West Coast of the United States. The distance showed 2,800 miles northward to Alaska and the Aleutians. The Solomons were 3,800 miles southwest and Tahiti was 2,700 miles to the south. It was enough to know that one could be lost on the map without venturing out on the sixty-eight million square miles of sea.

Nimitz emphasized this point in a future press conference when a young reporter asked him to speculate on when the war might end. He turned to the maps with a sweep of his hand. "By the calendar I wouldn't try to answer," he said, "but I can tell you by these maps. The war will end when the Japanese have been hunted down in all those regions and their striking power destroyed."

As Nimitz viewed the maps that morning he asked of the officer in charge, Lieutenant Charles Kirkpatrick, "What are those little numbers?" It seems the naval intelligence had devised a scheme of coding the ships according to types, units, and fleets by numbers. These were strategically placed on the map as to location; thus a particular set of numbers would look like: 46.13.4. This told the viewer at the headquarters at Pearl Harbor the exact location of each United States vessel. Naturally it was impossible for anyone and particularly the enemy to interpret the "little numbers" without the knowledge of the corresponding symbol index or codex.

Lieutenant Kirkpatrick quickly explained the system and its interpretation to Nimitz and then noted to his mates much later, "I never had to tell the new admiral anything twice. He got the formula the first time."

Nimitz began to count the number of men and supplies under his control. He needed to know the size of the nucleus that would grow to be the largest armada the world has ever known.

But he had to start practically from ground zero. The cool Texan with steel blue eyes put his mammoth mission into simple words. "I have just assumed a great responsibility with an underlying obligation which I shall do my utmost to discharge."

So began the work of Admiral Chester W. Nimitz, a fifty-seven-year-old master of strategy and tactics, at a time when the war was being won by the Japanese. From Pearl Harbor to Singapore the United States and Allied fleets were not hunting but were being hunted. Report after report came:

"WHERE IS THE NAVY?"

NIMITZ STAFF MEMBERS at Pearl Harbor in 1943: (left to Right) Vice Admirals William L. Calhoun, John H. Towers, Robert L. Ghormley, and Audrey W. Fitch.
— *Official U.S. Navy photo.*
Courtesy Admiral Nimitz State Historical Park

To this Nimitz did not reply. He decided during this period to give no interviews or hold any press conferences. To those whose querulous questions reached him, he would say in Hawaiian, *Hoomanawa nui* "—BE PATIENT!" To the public this seemed like a "cop out" and anything but encouraging. Only the navy secretary and the president understood.

The navy secretary was familiar with Nimitz's patience, a very special variety, which was Texas bred, and which bore no relationship to timidity. His colleagues never mistook Nimitz's kindness for weakness. Instead they considered it was power under full control. This control he needed as the next bulletin reached him:

SEVEN WARSHIPS: TWO TRANSPORTS
DOWN 22 DAMAGED — JAPANESE
VICTORY AT MAKASSAR STRAITS

Nimitz continued to avoid the press, nor would he talk with the public or issue statements of encouragement. There was no communication with the outside world as to the progress, if any, being made. Nimitz was holding the line and quietly building.

In addition, the Navy Department issued another announcement of responsibility to the already heavily burdened new admiral. They increased Nimitz's responsibility even further with an additional title: Commander-in-Chief of the Pacific Ocean Areas — CinCPOA!

When Nimitz took over the Pacific area, the Japanese had twice the number of battleships as the United States. They had over twice as many carriers. As a result, the American fleet was operating strictly from a defensive position. Nimitz had to fight a "holding war" with little to hold with. One of his admirals put it this way: "The crucial and critical time of the Pacific War will be when the Japanese attempt to take the North Pacific — and it will be necessary to husband every ounce of strength to meet the challenge. If we should fail in that challenge, the whole Pacific — and our West Coast — will be open to them."

This position was untenable. Nimitz realized he could not maintain any position long without additional help. For the first week he did nothing but study the exact components of his entire force. After that he began to build his fleet, his tactical strength, and his overall strategy.

During those first few months little was said but much was done. Quietly and without fanfare Nimitz worked. Major decisions were made. As Nimitz had expected, the first conflict was internal. The commanding officers and staff officers all had different approaches as to what should be done. These fell in two distinct divisions — those interested in operating battleships and those convinced aircraft carriers were the only means of success.

The effectiveness of a battleship in wartime had long been known and proven but the effectiveness of aircraft carriers remained to be tested. This type of warfare was initiated after World War I and until now had only been utilized in maneuvers. There were significant reasons, however, to make them essential components of task forces in the Pacific. This was going to be a total "all out" war and the air had to be defended as well as the sea. This strategy of bringing aircraft carriers into the Pacific needed to be coordinated with plans involving the field troops under the command of General Douglas MacArthur.

As the endless meetings of staff continued, it became evident that the tactics of the U.S. Fleet, in such vast waters, had to be similar to the Japanese approach at Pearl Harbor — by surprise. This would be very difficult since the Japanese were on the offensive. Nevertheless, a plan was laid out to invade the islands closest to Pearl Harbor. The Gilbert and the Marshall Islands were set up as initial targets for raiding expeditions.

This was not exactly Nimitz's way of operating. His strategy was to plot and plan carefully, taking all the time necessary to do the job once and for all. He continued to stave off the press as sharply as he gave orders — quietly but with emphasis. Nothing, absolutely nothing was coming out of CinCPac's headquarters.

Nimitz slept little and what sleep he did get was fretful. The war was not going well and Nimitz was helpless to turn it around.

Against all pressure to hurry and send out battleships in a concentrated raid, Nimitz held the line. The reason was obvious to the navy but unexplainable to the public. The ships were not ready. They were not adequately armed. They lacked sufficient fuel and were short on manpower.

Admiral King in Washington was getting impatient. The Asiatic fleet had retreated further south, past the Philippines into the Java Sea. In the Central Pacific the Japanese had advanced from the Marshall Islands to the Gilberts and northward with the appearance of preparing for a drive to the southwest from Ellice Island to Samoa. This drive was cause for immediate concern. All Japanese forces, aircraft, submarines, and carriers would be able to intercept shipping between the United States and Australia. This would close Australia to the United States as a potential base.

It also appeared that Midway was developing as the next potential Japanese target. Access there would bring another attack on Pearl Harbor. The next dispatch continued to be discouraging.

JAPANESE NAVY NOT A BATHTUB NAVY
DEFEAT IN JAVA SEA

Admiral King now pushed Nimitz to act. He recommended raids against the Gilberts and the Marshall Islands and offensive operations began to take shape.

Nimitz called in Vice Admiral William F. Halsey and asked for his counsel. Halsey was the epitome of a naval officer. Bushbrowed and powerfully built he came across gruff and impatient. Actually, he was soft-spoken and rarely swore, a fact few navy personnel believed. Halsey, like Nimitz, was mild mannered and courteous. His toughness was in his approach to the job and his short, cryptic commands: "Go get 'em" or "Whatever you do — do fast."

Halsey agreed completely with Nimitz concerning operations in the Gilbert and Marshall Islands. The following day, Nimitz accompanied Halsey to the wharf where they cleared the air for things to come.

Nimitz, a man of timing, asked Halsey, "Remember that meeting we had at the Waldorf in New York last year, Bill?"

Halsey couldn't help but smile, "How could I forget it. It's still funny, come to think of it."

The meeting in New York had been one that involved foreign dignitaries. Generals and admirals alike were in full dress uniform with lots of "scrambled eggs" on their caps and "fruit salad" on their chests.

Halsey had come out of the hotel and was waiting for the doorman to locate a cab. As Nimitz walked up behind him, a drunk approached from the opposite direction.

"Shay, doorman, get me a cab," he told Halsey.

The admiral was taken aback. Although not a tall man he straightened up to his full height and replied forcefully, "I'll have you know, sir, I am an admiral in the United States Navy."

"Zat's all right," the drunk replied. "Then get me a boat."

As Nimitz and Halsey reached the end of their walk, they were both smiling.

"Well, there's your 'boat', Bill!"

The tension was broken.

Nimitz wished Halsey good luck as the two friends shook hands. Halsey was on his way.

On January 11, the *Enterprise*, with Halsey in command, took three heavy cruisers, six destroyers, and one oiler out to sea. The next day the *Saratoga*, patrolling some 450 miles southwest of Oahu, was struck by a submarine torpedo and severely damaged, thus diminishing the force once again.

On schedule Halsey arrived off Samoa and waited for Admiral Fletcher and the *Yorktown* which had been delayed due to refueling problems. On January 25, the marines landed on Samoa under the cover of the *Enterprise* and *Yorktown* forces. In a matter of hours the radio dispatches began to come in. The enemy was being challenged.

TOTAL DESTRUCTION OF TWO SUBMARINES
ONE LIGHT CRUISER
ONE SMALL CARRIER
FOUR AUXILIARY
WIDE SPREAD DESTRUCTION
THIRTEEN PLANES
CRUISER CHESTER
ENTERPRISE DAMAGED

Despite the cheering crowd that met the returning ships, the raid had not gone well. They made little if any real impact on the aggressive attacks by the Japanese in other parts of the Pacific. There was serious trouble on the Bataan peninsula and the nearby island of Corregidor. The sum total of all the Allied efforts was hardly worth writing home about.

As the situation worsened Nimitz was called upon to offer greater support to the southwest areas both in the form of reinforcements and in strategy. This doubled his responsibility and diminished the concentration of forces from one area to another.

During the first three months of this war, heavy attacks made by the Japanese in the north, south central, and southwest Pacific areas made an impossible situation to move equipment and supplies. To have done so would have been suicide.

Nimitz quickly dispatched Admiral Pye to Washington to confer with Admiral King. In the meantime Halsey took the *Enterprise* and with the help of the *Lexington* and *Yorktown* raided Wake and Eniwetok. This double blow was designed to shock the Japanese and perhaps shift some of their forces around, weakening their aggressive thrust to the south.

A new dispatch indicated future problems for Nimitz.

GENERAL DOUGLAS MACARTHUR
DESIGNATED SUPREME COMMANDER,
ALLIED FORCES IN THE
SOUTHWEST PACIFIC AREA

There was little opportunity for Nimitz to capture the headlines. He shunned the press. There was little to report and what he could report was bad. The morale at the base was low enough; no need to scatter it around the world. Secondly, Nimitz was preparing for an announcement all his own, one that might put the navy back into operation and consequently in control.

Toward the end of May, word was leaked to the

THREE ADMIRALS (left to right) are Nimitz, King and Halsey, September 28, 1943.
— *Official U.S. Navy photo, courtesy Captain Roy C. Smith III, USNR (Ret.)*

newspeople that Nimitz was about to make a move. The leak came from the generally inaccessible Office of Chief of Naval Intelligence. A map was prepared on a daily basis in the office dealing with the probable location of the Japanese units and the whereabouts of U.S. naval forces. The maps indicated that a showdown was not far off — Midway to be exact.

ADMIRAL NIMITZ on inspection tour of Midway after the invasion.

— Official U.S. Navy photo

10

Midway To Victory

Battles are first won in the minds of men. This was never more clearly demonstrated than at the Battle of Midway. Admiral Nimitz pitted his shrewd calculating mind against Admiral Isoroku Yamamoto's logical determination and the battle was on.

At CinCPac headquarters Nimitz built his defense by bringing together the best team he could find to develop the winning plan necessary to fight under adverse circumstances. He believed the right men could come up with the right answers. To this end he called in Edwin T. Layton.

Nimitz had been observing Lieutenant Commander Layton since his arrival at Pearl Harbor and he liked the man's honesty. The initial impression had not been the best due to the deplorable situation. Layton had confessed a personal guilt for the disaster at Pearl Harbor. He had failed to foresee imminent danger in the Japanese efforts and was not prepared to warn Kimmel of the attack. Nimitz believed Layton was entitled to a second chance, and was reluctant to replace him in the early stages of the reorganization. Layton quickly justified the confidence in him as a strategist by his predictions in the Coral Sea conflict which was the first naval action after Pearl Harbor. Layton accurately predicted the enemy maneuvers and strength at a crucial time.

Layton had distinct qualifications needed during this period of history. America had never been at war with Japan or involved in conflict at a time when aircraft carriers were a factor in naval warfare. These two factors presented a new type of strategy. Fortunately Layton had served in Japan. He knew the language and the customs of the people. Also as a student of psychology he understood the Japanese mind and behavior and could more authentically predict and describe motivations. Now that he had the opportunity of serving in the Pacific area of combat with a detailed knowledge of the movements of the entire Japanese naval forces, he was ideal for interpreting the strategy and tactics of Yamamoto.

Nimitz's next step was to call in Lieutenant Commander Joseph J. Rochefort.

Joe Rochefort was one of the first men Nimitz met on his arrival in the islands. The lieutenant commander had shown him around the Naval District's Combat Intelligence Unit that was humorously dubbed "Hypo." Rochefort was in charge of this complex communication center which had a direct radio connection with Washington, Corregidor, and the British alliance in Singapore. His duty was mainly to analyze traffic, locate and track transmitters, and decode the messages through cryptanalysis. Actually, cryptanalysis was Rochefort's specialty and in particular the Japanese navy's operational code. When Nimitz had first viewed the communications headquarters, he was not impressed.

CIRCLE DRIVE, flag officers' quarters on Guam during World War II.
— *Official U.S. Navy photo.*
Courtesy Admiral Nimitz State Historical Park

His unexpressed thoughts were, if this was such a great operation why did they let Kimmel down when he needed them most?

But today was a new day. Nimitz needed Rochefort's ability to unscramble the Japanese CODE JN25 quickly and without error. The CODE JN25 consisted of 45,000 five-digit groups that represented complex words and phrases. The key to any decodification was the capability of locating and translating the same numbers in a random group, subtracting them and comparing them to the code book. It was no job for an inexperienced sailor.

Knowing the Japanese mind and knowing how to unscramble messages were both primary to strategy. Nimitz was convinced that sound strategy is based on knowledge, information, and technical experience. Together this small team was to put their skills to work and develop and execute the first major thrust of the United States force in the Pacific. Nimitz's ability to pick the man for the job could not fail him now. America could not tolerate another fatal blow.

The CinCPac team was in place. Nimitz knew perfectly well the enemy was aware of the United States' building program. They also knew in time the U.S. forces would be sufficiently strong to take the offensive. In the meantime, Nimitz's fleet was vulnerable. His forces were inadequate and could not bear the risk of a loss. Yet he delayed as long as possible the time of aggressive action and now must take the offensive.

Layton and Rochefort had apprised Nimitz of the latest Japanese dispatch. On May 1 a coded communique had informed them that the Japanese Imperial Headquarters had issued an order to the commander-in-chief's combined fleet, in cooperation with the army, to invade and occupy strategic points in the western Aleutians.

These were the long string of islands extending from the point of Alaska in the northern Pacific. Midway and Wake were south of there. Nevertheless these islands were opportune to future advances by the Japanese — a strategy they called the "ribbon defense." Midway was needed as a base for air raids on Pearl Harbor and San Francisco. But even more Yamamoto wanted a point from which he could draw out the American fleet and annihilate it before construction could restore the losses encountered at Pearl Harbor. But where exactly would they attack?

In early May Rochefort's team intercepted several radio messages using a mysterious AF code name. The team knew it was the name of a place but

USS Alabama 1942. An example of WWII camouflage on the high seas.
— *Official U.S. Navy photo.*
Courtesy Admiral Nimitz State Historical Park

Rochefort was uncertain of its identity. Nimitz and Rochefort both knew it was important in revealing where the Japanese might strike next. Rochefort made several attempts at finding out but all efforts failed. He and Layton and their assistant, Lieutenant Jasper Holmes, then decided to trick the Japanese.

Since the undersea cable was still into Midway they directed the island to send a radio message in plain English saying that their fresh water distillation plant was malfunctioning.

The plot worked. Within forty-eight hours the code breakers picked up a message from the Japanese naval radio on Wake: AF without water. This gave Nimitz all of the information he needed. A major Japanese invasion would be launched against Midway.

Immediately Nimitz confronted Layton. "Layton, you have now become the enemy. I want you to be Yamamoto. Probe his mind. Find out what he is thinking. Get under his skin. Know him inside and out and report back to me the time, the place, and the hour he will strike. I'm calling Halsey."

Nimitz spent the next few days pulling his best ships back to port. Halsey was still somewhere in the Coral Sea but was ordered to return immediately. Fletcher, with the *Yorktown,* was due any time, crippled and almost to the breaking point. There was so little to work with.

But the shortage of ships was not Nimitz's only problem. Halsey was sick. When the *Enterprise* docked Halsey stepped off the deck weak, feverish, and a bundle of nerves. Undue stress had taken its toll. A skin infection had broken out all over his body and Halsey could do nothing but go to the hospital. This left the problem of finding a replacement for him.

Halsey recommended Rear Admiral Raymond A. Spruance, saying he was "a cold-blooded fighting fool like David Dixon Porter" the famous Civil War admiral. Halsey knew he possessed a sound, computer-type mind and a clear philosophy of battle. Spruance advocated for supreme naval strategy to be the "use of all the weapons that you have at your command." He was an all-out combateer. Spruance was given the *Enterprise* group.

Altogether Nimitz did not have the fleet or the weapons to compete. The odds were against him and it was to be a lopsided battle at best.

Yamamoto was an intelligent officer. He reasoned soundly and with a single purpose in mind. Yamamoto believed that if he could conquer Midway there would be nothing left between him and San Francisco that would challenge Japan and he would have a chance to finish off the Pacific fleet damaged at Pearl Harbor.

Layton paralleled his thinking. Yamamoto would strike first at Dutch Harbor at the tip of Alaska; then he would attack Midway. He reasoned the Dutch Harbor attack would bring forces from the coast and Pearl Harbor in order to defend Alaska. The attack on Midway should draw out all remaining forces and he would have the chance he wanted — the destruction of American sea power.

This made sense when the figures involved were evaluated. Reliable sources indicated that Yamamoto had 162 warships at his disposal. They presented a balanced attacking unit with strong battleship support, large and small aircraft carriers, a mixture of heavy and light cruisers, a proportionate number of destroyers, along with large transports that were protected, in part, by a fleet of submarines. The many small patrol craft were not included in this number.

The American fleet, on the other hand, consisted of 76 warships, but one-third of them were assigned to the North Pacific fleet and never got into battle. Nimitz actually had less than 50 ships to work with. His forces included three aircraft carriers with about 230 planes. These were supported by 32 Navy Catalinas, six new torpedo Avenger bombers, 54 Marine Corps planes and 23 Army Air Force planes, 19 of which were land based B-17s. The challenge to Nimitz was to make them all work for him.

Despite the imbalance and apparent underdog position Nimitz held the trump card. He knew the attack was to be at Midway and this provided an advantage Yamamoto was not reckoning with. Also Nimitz was patiently and quietly gathering his forces and on May 28 he set his strategy in motion.

To Fletcher and Spruance he challenged: "Inflict maximum damage on the enemy by employing strong attrition tactics." Privately he counseled with them to be careful. The men were like brothers and there was more than professional orders that were exchanged. There was a genuine pact that passed between them. To all his commanders at sea he then ordered, "You will be governed by the principle of calculated risk which you will interpret to mean the avoidance of exposure of your force from attack by superior enemy forces without good prospect of inflicting greater damage on the enemy."

Nimitz had learned through the years that "horses pull harder when the reins lie loose." He gave an order; then relied on his men to do what they thought best under a given situation.

Nimitz quickly had his fleet move out and set them on a course to a point northeast of Midway where they could flank the Japanese as they came in from the northwest. On the other side of the Pacific four huge carriers, the *Soryu,* the *Hiryu,* the *Kaga* and the *Akagi,* all veterans of Pearl Harbor, under the command of Admiral Chuichi Nagumo, were advancing under a heavy cloud cover. Admiral Yamamoto's main force was lagging some distance behind. The second force under the command of Vice Admiral Boshiro Hosogaya was coming from the southwest. Vice Admiral Shiru Takasu was leading a screen force. Finally, the transports, the minesweepers, and the heavy cruisers were gliding gracefully into target range from Saipan, Guam, and from Japan itself. There was no doubt that the Japanese had decided to invade Midway and make it a port of departure from which to attack Hawaii again. Thinking they would be attacking Midway as they had done at Pearl Harbor, under full surprise, they had their submarines set up in two picket lines halfway between Hawaii and Midway Island. This would allow them to intercept the American fleet as they were drawn out from Pearl Harbor to defend Midway.

It was a neat plan. But Nimitz had outsmarted them.

Day and night Rochefort and his team had worked piecing together the many long-range radio dispatches from the Japanese in an effort to understand their plan of attack on Midway. Their careers depended on its accuracy. More importantly, so did the lives of the men comprising the U.S. Fleet. Layton and the Nimitz's Fleet Intelligence Unit were more meticulous than ever. They pored over maps, studied weather charts and wind currents. No detail was overlooked. A scientist at work over a microscope could not have been more minute in his scrutiny of data. Carefully and cautiously he plotted the movement of the Japanese vessels. So it was not surprising that a few short hours before the Japanese submarines arrived at their destined rendezvous between the two islands, the United States fleet had glided through leaving them free to proceed to Midway unmolested. Even more significantly the enemy strategy was canceled because Yamamoto was relying upon the submarines to be the eyes of the fleet in finding the enemy.

Layton was then ordered to give Nimitz his plan in detail. "As admiral of the Japanese fleet what are you going to do?" Nimitz asked him.

"All right, here it is," said Layton. "The carriers commanded by Nagumo will attack Midway on the morning of the 4th. They will come from the northwest on a bearing of 325 degrees and will be

USS *YORKTOWN* crew as they watch the destruction of a Japanese "Kate" torpedo bomber during the assault on the Gilbert Islands.
— *Official U.S. Navy photo.
Courtesy Admiral Nimitz State Historical Park*

USS *MISSOURI* shown firing her main batteries during World War II. Later the peace treaty with Japan was signed on this same deck.
— *Official U.S. Navy photo.
Courtesy Admiral Nimitz State Historical Park*

sighted about 175 miles from Midway about 5 o'clock in the morning."

Nimitz flashed his approving smile. "The course is set. This time we are not waiting for Yamamoto — we will strike first. We will establish a 'ribbon defense' of our own — all the way to Tokyo." Heading confidently toward Midway was Task Force 16 with Admiral Spruance commanding two carriers, the *Enterprise* and the *Hornet*, six cruisers, and nine destroyers. The hastily-patched *Yorktown* under the command of Admiral Fletcher with two cruisers and six destroyers followed proudly behind.

Gradually through the long night of June 3 the American armada and the Japanese forces quietly converged upon each other. Shortly before dawn a Midway search plane came upon part of the Japanese minesweepers coming up from the southwest. The pilot also reported two cargo ships sighted five hundred miles out. Less than half an hour later another patrol plane reported six ships, again coming from the southwest. It was the morning of June 4. The time was 5 a.m.

Layton's predictions were on target!

Suddenly, Japanese planes of all kinds came up over the horizon. There were dive bombers, torpedo planes, and protecting Zeros, 108 of them in all, which sped through the morning sky toward their destination. A second flight of bombers were warming up on the carrier flight decks where the lighter planes had come from.

When the Midway search radar picked up the Japanese squadron ninety-three miles away the little band of defenders prepared for the onslaught. Fifteen of the twenty-five marine pilots bravely took off in their obsolete planes to challenge the modern Japanese aircraft. At the same time seventy-two torpedo bombers roared outward from the decks of the *Hornet* and the *Yorktown* headed for the enemy carriers. The naval might of two maritime powers was converging head-on.

Attack, attack, attack!

Back at CinCPac Rochefort remained in his stuffy underground station. Nimitz stayed in his office and often rested on a cot when he could while Layton covered the outer office. Constant communication flowed between the two headquarters. All reports were immediately analyzed. Nimitz, the man of stern discipline, waited anxiously. For the first two hours after daybreak the reports were scant. Only Japanese radio messages arrived — most of which could not be immediately decoded. Obviously they had made some radical changes at a late hour. Admiral Nagumo on the flagship *Akagi* had thought of everything.

The next communique came in plain English.

TEN ENEMY TORPEDO PLANES
HEADING TOWARD US!

Layton told Nimitz, "These have to be from U.S. carriers. Nagumo was either completing the launching of his reserve aircraft, or he was recovering his planes from Midway. The latter seemed more likely. This would mean Nagumo would not be able to launch again for two hours. A good time for dive bombers."

But the fleet's reports were slow.

"What are they doing out there?" Nimitz demanded impatiently of Layton.

"Give 'em time, sir, give them time."

Suddenly around ten o'clock the messages began coming and CinCPac knew Midway was being bombed heavily.

TORPEDO 8 LOST EVERY PLANE — EVERY MAN MIDWAY SUFFERS LOSS: FUEL TANKS,

HANGARS SEAPLANE RAMPS, BARRACKS, MESS HALL, GALLEY ON MIDWAY DESTROYED 33 TORPEDO PLANES DOWN

The reports were devastating. Nimitz shivered the shiver of fear. The Japanese appeared to be winning. So far the U.S. had lost thirty-three torpedo planes and the Japanese fleet had not even been scratched. The dark hour of despair gripped Nimitz. He was aware that if the Japanese won Midway the war would be theirs. He began to wonder if his strategy had been wrong or had he been too arrogant in believing his rebuilt fleet could withstand such powerful opposition? The commander paced up and down the room like a restless animal.

Suddenly Lady Luck came to the aid of the beleaguered Americans. Low on gas, a group of SBD dive bombers turned and followed a Japanese destroyer going at flank speed across the Pacific hoping it would lead them to the carriers. The guess was good and the luck was holding because four carriers were sighted at a time when they were the most vulnerable. Their decks were covered with torpedoes, bombs, and refueled aircraft. When the Zeros protecting them were all at sea level shooting down the unfortunate torpedo bombers, the Dauntless dive bombers struck.

The American pilots found pay dirt. They repeatedly pounded the carriers with bombs and open fire. Instantly flames, fire, and rapid explosions followed. Before the Japanese knew what had hit them flames shot up from the carriers' superstructures and repeated explosions gutted the interior of the ships.

The *Akagi* was wrecked within minutes and scuttled the next day. Admiral Nagumo abandoned his flagship and moved the survivors to a nearby cruiser.

The *Kaga's* captain was killed on the bridge as explosions blew out the ship's belly.

Minutes later the *Soryu* exploded and began sinking that fateful day. The *Hiriu* was blasted into a hulk and was scuttled on June 5. The course of victory had been snatched out of the hands of the enemy. In five minutes the backbone of the Japanese navy had been broken, and the course of the Pacific war was turned.

As Nimitz relaxed for the first time as he listened to the news, he couldn't help but remember his days at the Academy when he was studying other battles, especially the Battle of Lake Erie. It was there that Commodore Oliver H. Perry had outmaneuvered the British during the War of 1812 and brought about an important American victory at a time when it was most needed. He recalled the words Perry sent to the American commander: "We have met the enemy and they are ours." Nimitz was about to share his thoughts with Layton when a communique came:

THE ENEMY FLEET WHICH HAS BEEN PRACTICALLY DESTROYED IS RETURNING TO THE EAST. COMBINED FLEET UNITS IN THE VICINITY ARE PREPARING TO PURSUE THE REMNANTS AND AT THE SAME TIME OCCUPY MIDWAY!

Layton pointed out to Nimitz what possibly was happening — Yamamoto might be bringing up the main force to land at Midway.

Instead the Japanese admiral, as a last ditch effort, attempted to lure Task Force 16 into the range of the shore-based Japanese aircraft at Wake Island but failed. Spruance's forces were running low on fuel and fortunately cut back to the east. Yamamoto

ADMIRAL NIMITZ presenting awards for bravery to officers and men on board the USS Submarine *Grayling*.
— *Official U.S. Navy photo.
Courtesy Admiral Nimitz State Historical Park*

was forced to turn tail in an historic admission of failure:

OCCUPATION OF MIDWAY IS CANCELED!

The battle of Midway was over.

Nimitz declared to Layton: "This battle may be the greatest sea battle since Jutland." But then he began to count its cost.

The United States had lost the *Yorktown* and one destroyer. The Japanese had lost four carriers and a heavy cruiser. A battleship and two destroyers were damaged. The Americans lost 150 planes — the Japanese 322. There were 307 American servicemen killed and 3,500 Japanese, many of them their country's finest pilots.

Nimitz told Layton, "We have come away winners in more ways than one. We have learned that the battleship is limited and can only be used to provide cover for invasion forces. We have learned we need faster and lighter aircraft with quicker climbing power and maneuverability." He also suggested to Rochefort, "Communication methods need to be updated using superfrequency voice sets for direct voice communication."

Then to both men he offered his hand.

"TODAY, GENTLEMEN, PEARL HARBOR HAS BEEN REVENGED!"

11

The War Behind The War

As the initial glow of victory began to fade pilots from all branches of the service began to evaluate their contributions in turning the tide in the Pacific. In reality, every man, regardless of service affiliation, could claim a vital role in the outcome.

In Washington, General George Marshall exclaimed to the president, "It was the closest squeak and the greatest victory."

It was more than that. It was a disaster for the Japanese from which they never recovered. They were never again to take the offensive in "American" waters.

The victory of Midway did not, however, delude Nimitz. He knew perfectly well that difficult days lay ahead. The Japanese still dominated the southwest Pacific. In the last several months they had occupied Singapore and Malaysia, Sumatra and the Celebes, the Bismarck Archipelago, and had severely damaged Port Darwin in Australia. Amid all the newspaper and radio reports throughout the country on how the Midway battle was won, Nimitz gave credit where credit was rightfully due. When congratulating a submarine commander for destroying three enemy ships on a given day, he said, "When the subs hit them, they go down for the count." The commander relayed the message to his crew. The reaction was high jubilation as the commander said, "It was like God had spoken."

It was at times like this that Chester Nimitz was at his best. The drama of Midway had taught him many things. He was determined to go into an offensive position as soon as possible.

The very nature of the task brought together the finest qualities of the Nimitz mind. Any mixture of confusion and doubt evaporated and a clear plan emerged that was rapidly translated into a future action. Though an intense commitment to the naval system of operations was followed Nimitz was creative enough to keep an open mind. It was very important to him that all possibilities be examined. All options brought to his attention became alternatives if they were sound and workable. He knew that often the best ideas didn't come from the top, but often from the men in the forefront of battle; from the men flying the planes, the men releasing the bombs and manning the carriers.

Although demands on him were heavy, Nimitz took the time to confer with the men returning from battle. He asked them what they thought, how they felt, and what suggestions they might have.

Nimitz became known as a man who was accessible to his men. He was so accessible that one day while making his ten-mile walk on one of the beaches in Hawaii he inadvertently stepped on a sailor who was enjoying a little rest and relaxation on the beach. The young man had covered himself with sand and was napping. The admiral didn't see him nor the sailor the admiral. When the admiral's foot landed on the sailor he instinctively yelled "ouch" and then seeing who it was, quickly added, "sir."

Nimitz was quick to reply, "Sorry, I *thought* this beach was a little bumpy."

To carry out the desired offensive Nimitz needed to:

1. Restructure the chain of command for coordinating airpower in the Pacific area of operations.
2. As Fleet Admiral he needed to assume the customary role in Washington for the Pacific's share of men, arms, and supplies.
3. Participate in the final decision in Washington and help design the strategy for movement across the Pacific and the ultimate invasion of Japan.

It wasn't long before Nimitz was ready to make some rather earth-shaking announcements on command structure and reassignment of priorities that would affect the entire naval operation in the Pacific.

At the same time the Japanese were also rethinking their plans. They had incurred heavy damage to their fleet and had taken an unexpected thrashing at the hands of the American navy. Admiral Yamamoto retreated to the South Pacific to concentrate on new strategy. It was no coincidence that both Nimitz and Yamamoto were pinpointing their new targets toward Tulagi and Guadalcanal.

Guadalcanal was the largest island in the Solomons, and a British possession since World War I. It was significant to both nations since it provided a gateway to Australia and direct access to Japan. The Japanese had often said that the Solomon Islands were like a ladder leading toward Japan. Guadalcanal was the bottom rung of that ladder.

If the Unites States could secure that island the

American forces might climb all the way to the Japanese mainland.

In Australia General Douglas MacArthur was also scrutinizing the Midway reports. His suggestion to Admiral King was that the American forces invade and secure Rabaul immediately. He offered to execute this action and boasted that he could accomplish it with one amphibiously trained division if the navy would lend him support by carrier aircraft.

Nimitz was not convinced. This plan would mean committing fast carriers and since there were then only two in the Solomon area, Nimitz feared MacArthur might regard the carriers as "expendable." He had no intentions of taking that risk by jeopardizing them in such an ambitious undertaking. The gamble would be too great. King, Nimitz, and their staffs considered an amphibious assault on Rabaul to be about as sensible at that time as ordering lead soldiers to storm a red-hot stove. They all opposed the plan. It was agreed, however, from the president on down, that something must be done to check the Japanese. Admiral King and Nimitz concurred that the Tulagi and Guadalcanal areas were where they should begin. The code name for this operation would be *Watchtower*.

There remained the thorny problem of command. Actually, Nimitz was more knowledgeable of the problem of air command than the pilots thought. Immediately after Midway he had requested authority from Washington to assign air force commanders and suggested Rear Admiral Aubrey W. Fitch as commander of the *Lexington* task force. At this time Rear Admiral John S. McCain requested an air force brigadier general, if he could have one, to assist him in air operations in the South Pacific.

Nimitz agreed that army aircraft in the South Pacific should be permanently assigned to bases. Without a lot of luck it was too much to expect to move aircraft to threatened points and get effective use.

General George Marshall wanted MacArthur to conduct the march up the Solomons and in this case MacArthur wanted the navy under his own command. Vice Admiral Arthur S. Carpender filled that slot and King insisted the first phase of *Watchtower* be run by the navy — as the forces to be employed consisted entirely of naval and marine personnel. The announcement was then made of subsequent assignments. Ghormley would be in command and in charge of strategy. Fletcher would serve as tactical officer afloat. Rear Admiral Richmond Kelly Turner would direct the amphibious operation and Major General A. A. Vandegrift of the marines would command the troops ashore with McCain's planes operating out of bases in his area.

In the reassignments contingent to these plans, Major General Harmon, an army airman, was nonplussed and complained to Nimitz when McCain was to be in charge of the air strikes for these operations. Nimitz with a grin quickly said to Harmon, "I feel sure you will work *HARMONiously* with each other." The pun worked and the assignments proceeded as planned. Nimitz's sense of humor again won the day.

In the summer of 1942 the name of Chester W. Nimitz was not a household word. It was just beginning to emerge with such names as MacArthur and Eisenhower as men destined to become legends in their own time.

Before the war became history, however, Admiral Nimitz was to engage in years of agonizing and intensely demanding conflict, not only with the enemy, but with contrasting interests and commitments from Washington to be added to the decisions he must make as commander in the Pacific. Mingled in this were many vignettes of interest. One of these surrounded a trip he was preparing to make to San Francisco by air to confer with Admiral King.

The first member of Congress to join the service after war was declared was serving in New Guinea and developed dengue fever. He was flown to Pearl Harbor to recuperate. Nimitz became aware of the congressman's presence in the hospital and ordered the best of care for him. When the flight was scheduled for San Francisco Nimitz offered him a seat on his plane. The young congressman refused with regret, stating he just didn't feel up to the trip.

Just as the amphibian plane was about to touch down at San Francisco it struck a floating log. The bow shot up and the entire plane flipped over with a hole torn in the hull. Inside the cabin bodies were hurtled through the air. Immediately the plane began to fill with water and all able-bodied personnel scrambled for an open freight hatch and they clambered out on what had been the wing of the plane. A rescue boat was soon at the scene and medics began examining those seriously hurt. Nimitz and Mercer, his aide, were fortunate to escape serious injury due to the fact that they had been seated with their backs toward the front. Nimitz was hurting, but mobile. He yelled at Mercer to retrieve the briefcase with the reports on Midway and then began helping the injured out of the plane into the rescue boat. All except Nimitz and Mercer had broken bones. One of the pilots had been killed. It was a near disaster for Nimitz on his first return to the mainland since Pearl Harbor.

The young congressman might well have given thanks that he had been unable to make the trip that day. Lyndon B. Johnson took a later flight after his recovery and the young officer who had taken his place was drowned.

The second week in July, Nimitz ordered Ghormley to Melbourne, Australia, to confer with MacArthur. Together they were to finalize the plans for Tulagi and Guadalcanal. MacArthur was gracious but arbitrary and demanding. Ghormley left discouraged and reported to Nimitz that the target date for *Watchtower* must now be pushed back to August 7. Nimitz agreed and the operation *Watchtower* moved forward.

Early on the morning of the seventh, shore bombardment began from Fletcher's fleet. Their task was to smash defenses ashore and to provide cover for the landing of the first of many waves of marines who would make the initial assault. Nimitz wired King in Washington — "at least we have started."

Then began what was to be one of the bitterest campaigns in the entire war. There was very little fighting on Guadalcanal the first few days and then it broke out with an intensity that was both demanding and devastating.

Admiral Yamamoto realizing the challenge now at stake committed his largest force since Midway to the area: three carriers, three battleships, nine cruisers, thirteen destroyers, thirty-six submarines, and several auxiliaries. Not knowing the full extent of the marine and army forces on Guadalcanal he also ordered night delivery runs consisting of troops, ammunition, and supplies down the "Slot," an island flanked from Bougainville to Guadalcanal. These runs became known as the "Tokyo Express."

These nightly reinforcements increased the strength of the enemy and depleted the American forces appreciably. While the enemy numbers were increasing on the island the American marines were placed in an extremely vulnerable position. A double jeopardy developed when Admiral Turner was forced to withdraw his entire fleet from Guadalcanal because of a fuel shortage. This left the marines desolate — without reinforcements, and much needed food and medical supplies. Later these were brought in by naval ships at considerable cost. It placed them in grave danger of losing what they had so recently gained. The American flag flew over Guadalcanal but the marine forces were beleagured. The question was, could they hold on?

Miraculously the marines were holding on to a tiny strip of land, an area about nine miles long and three miles wide. General Vandegrift wanted to move further into the island but he lacked the men and supplies to support the action.

Every night the Japanese blasted them with bombs and gunfire, both from offshore batteries and from the ground troops being continually supplied by a nightly run of the "Tokyo Express."

Nimitz decided he must observe the combat zone himself and personally evaluate the situation. He radioed MacArthur and invited the general to join him at Ghormley's headquarters at Noumea, New Caledonia. MacArthur replied with a counter invitation for Nimitz to come to Brisbane. Nimitz declined. MacArthur sent representatives to Noumea.

When Nimitz arrived at Noumea he called an immediate staff meeting. Everyone was to make a report of what they perceived to be the problem. Ghormley's report was pessimistic. He did not believe the American forces were strong enough to withstand the onslaught of the Japanese around-the-clock attacks. The rest of the staff concurred. Nimitz's word to them from Washington was there would be no more troops available soon and they would have to do the best they could. Nimitz left with instructions to Ghormley to come up with a more positive approach as soon as possible and report to him. He then boarded his plane for Guadalcanal.

Landing the next day on Guadalcanal Nimitz was met by a lively and gregarious General Vandegrift. Immediately he noticed a difference in attitude. The closer he came to the combat zone the more optimistic the officers and men were. Ghormley and MacArthur seemed to be the only negative thinkers. General Vandegrift and his marines showed unbelievable confidence. "Are you going to hold this beachhead, General?" asked Nimitz.

"Hell yes," Vandegrift shot back, "Why not?"

Vandegrift was a man after Nimitz's own heart. Nimitz pledged his best support and headed back to Pearl Harbor more encouraged than he had been the day before.

As soon as Nimitz arrived at Pearl Harbor he notified Washington. He reported to King the grave situation and immediate peril. He insisted that the marines could continue to hold Guadalcanal if reinforcements came and came quickly.

At the time, the American army was planning the invasion of North Africa, and men and supplies were being directed en masse to that area.

Fortunately, President Roosevelt recognized the logic in the request by Nimitz for more help in the Pacific and took a direct hand in the decision-making. Alarmed by the ferocious fighting and the thin line of defense he ordered heavy reinforcements to be directed immediately to the Solomons.

This done Nimitz had his own adjustment to take care of. He called his staff and made the announcement, "This critical condition requires a more aggressive commander." And in spite of his personal friendship and deep regard for the man it was no surprise that Nimitz announced the appointment of the most aggressive commander of them all, Admiral Bill Halsey, to take over Admiral Ghormley's command. Guadalcanal and Vandegrift deserved the right man and Nimitz knew the man. So on October 18, Admiral Halsey read his new instructions: YOU WILL TAKE COMMAND OF THE SOUTH PACIFIC AREA AND SOUTH PACIFIC FORCES IMMEDIATELY.

It was not a moment too soon. The news of Halsey's appointment spread like an oil slick throughout the beachhead and if it did nothing else it immediately brought new heart and spirit to the fighting men in the Solomons.

In his own cryptic, inflammable way he created excitement and enthusiasm and surged new hope into the tired and sick marines, who were valiantly holding on. Halsey, never one to be misunderstood, said what he meant and meant what he said. When he cried out, "Kill Japs, then kill more Japs," he had but one objective in mind. His own enthusiasm ignited the weary forces in Guadalcanal.

Almost before Halsey could settle down at the Noumea headquarters Nimitz ordered him to prepare a naval attack on *Watchtower*, to be executed early in November. Without hesitation Halsey issued an all-out naval alert and immediately rushed new troops into the area under the escort of Admiral Turner's convoy.

On November 12 the Americans waited in ambush in Ironbottom Sound after night had fallen. In spite of radar devices they were surprised, however, when the Japanese force entered the Sound shortly after midnight. The ensuing battle set off one of the bloodiest confrontations of the South Pacific war. In less than thirty minutes ships from both sides blasted away at each other hitting whatever they

NATIVE POLICE BOY in New Guinea draws a map on the ground showing the position of native forces, November 15, 1942.

— *Official U.S. Navy photo.*
Courtesy Admiral Nimitz State Historical Park

could in the dark. The result was severe damage to both sides. Every participating United States ship was hit: the *Atlanta* was sunk, the cruiser *Portland* was rendered powerless, and the crippled *Juneau* was sunk by a submarine sending 700 crew members to their death. The Japanese likewise lost two destroyers and the battleship *Hiei* was bombarded repeatedly until sunk.

By morning Turner had gotten his convoy through and the Japanese had temporarily turned back giving the Americans the victory over the first phase of the naval battle of Guadalcanal. In the days ahead there were other battles, hard fought and with heavy losses, but by the middle of November the tide of battle in the Solomons was favoring the United States. The direct challenge of the island was over but Japan was not willing to declare defeat. One more battle was to be fought off Tassafaronga Point that resulted in a Japanese victory, but it was too late. The Americans had already achieved a naval supremacy and continued to build up troop support until they gradually outnumbered the enemy.

By late December, the 1st Marine Division was withdrawn, at least what was left of it, and the Americans went through the daily routine of dislodging Japanese soldiers, sick and without supplies, on a one-to-one basis. Defensive to the end the Japanese were indefatigable diggers and burrowers and would hole up and hold out in foxholes until the opportunity to die only when they could take an American with them.

It was days before the empire quietly granted concession. But gradually they evacuated their troops and left the island to the Americans. It was a strange victory. Operation *Watchtower* had come to a successful, but costly, end. At Guadalcanal, as at Midway, the Americans had started out weaker and on the defensive and had come out winners.

Over the dial face of the calendar it was December 31 and Nimitz noted in his letter to Catherine, it was also the end of the first year at Pearl Harbor.

It had been a hard year.

12

1943

Back at Pearl Harbor Nimitz was pleased over the outcome of the struggle of Guadalcanal but was decidedly distressed at the heavy casualties. It took the lives of 1,600 marines and army troops along with thousands of sailors. It took an even greater toll of the enemy — a loss that sent the Japanese reeling back to their homeland to reevaluate their position. On this island alone, 15,000 of their men died in battle and over 9,000 died of tropical diseases. The loss to both countries would be felt for years to come.

Nimitz took the loss personally, vowing to do all he could to insure that future confrontations would be more favorable for the United States. On many occasions Nimitz took the time to write to families in the states about men who had fought for islands few Americans had heard of prior to the war. It helped some, but it didn't bring back the boys.

Even though the marines had taken Guadalcanal Nimitz was not in the mood to celebrate. In the first place he was coming down with malaria, a dis-

DAWN LANDING ON Wake Island — Silhouetted by the sun, American soldiers wade ashore through waist-high surf to storm Wake Island on May 16, 1944.
— *Official U.S. Navy photo.*
Courtesy Admiral Nimitz State Historical Park

A KINGFISHER observation plane used by American forces from battleships and cruisers. — *Official U.S. Navy photo.*
Courtesy Admiral Nimitz State Historical Park

ease he, no doubt, encountered while island hopping a few weeks earlier. Added to this was MacArthur's wave making about his new approach to "finishing off the Japanese."

Without counseling with other commanders of the area, MacArthur suggested to the Joint Chiefs of Staff in Washington a complete strategy for defeating the Japanese. He proposed that, since Guadalcanal had been captured, the transpacific advance on Japan should be executed upward to New Guinea and the Philippines by his own forces. Being an army general, this drive, he insisted, must be mainly an army offensive. The naval forces would be used to carry the men, in a series of coastal leaps, to the various islands under the cover of army aircraft.

Nimitz regarded this proposal as preposterous —another MacArthurism. It was no wonder Nimitz kept a picture of the general on his desk at Pearl Harbor. He said it was to remind him "not to make Jovian pronouncements complete with thunderbolts." This plan made the navy nothing more than valets for the army and he would have none of it. Nimitz believed he had a better plan. He argued that MacArthur's approach to Japan was round about, uneconomical use of men and supplies, and required too much time. His plan, on the other hand, sent the navy, army, and marines directly across the central part of the Pacific. Here there were no land masses, only hundreds of small islands and atolls providing a choice of targets, and numerous alternatives for landing strips and bases of operation.

Early in the war months, Nimitz, being a student of naval history and strategy, remembered that the navy anticipated the Central Pacific move to be the best approach to use the twenty-two new fleet carriers, ordered years before by Congress. They were now coming out of the shipyards and had been directed to Pearl Harbor. Naturally, he pushed and pushed hard for his operation to be selected by the Joint Chiefs of Staff and their subcommittees. When the word finally came down from Washington, they had accepted Nimitz's plan and he felt justified in his own mind.

MacArthur vigorously protested but was unable to dissuade the higher authority. It was therefore agreed to open a Central Pacific axis as the main line of advance against Japan, and General MacArthur would continue his advance from the south.

Fortunately, the first three months of 1943 were relatively calm. Both sides were licking their wounds and counting their heavy losses. Certainly, Premier Hideki Tojo, chief architect of the Japanese forces, had to reexamine his country's position. For the Allied forces the interim was used as a time to replan, recoup, and assess small victories among the tiny islands that dotted the large and awesome expanse of the Pacific.

It was a time for Nimitz to pass out accolades and do the honors of an admiral. On one occasion a young lieutenant was being awarded the Navy Cross and as Nimitz pinned the medal on his chest he looked up at him and asked, "You're from Texas, aren't you?" "Yes, sir," the lieutenant replied. "I thought so," said Nimitz. The admiral had always said he would never ask a man if he was from Texas if he didn't think he was. He didn't want to embarrass him.

The time was also spent in evaluation. Every two months Admiral King and Admiral Nimitz usually met in San Francisco with their chiefs of staff for a Cominch-CinCPac conference. Admiral Forrest P. Sherman attended with Nimitz. At that time every admiral was evaluated for his performance. Often Admiral King was critical, caustic, and belligerent. He was inclined to pull the men from the field for the slightest provocation. Nimitz, with his quiet power, took up for his people. Often he would react to King by saying, "If something is wrong with him, you had better start looking at me." And the rough moment was over. Through those hard moments of planning, both for strategy and personnel, never was one situation overlooked or one person neglected. Regardless of the time it took, the two admirals did their job.

Nimitz settled back at Pearl Harbor to assess his own situation. He considered himself a team man and was comfortable with it. He was particularly indisposed, however, to grant MacArthur his way as so many people were, especially if it had political overtones. Nimitz knew public pressure and sentiment was being brought to bear in MacArthur's favor. The headlines on the homefronts regularly featured MacArthur and this endeared him to the people. The press was making him a national hero. His defense of the Philippines and his dramatic promise to return inspired the mothers and fathers and they sang his praises throughout the land.

Nimitz, along with the Joint Chiefs of Staff, thought the dual drive in the Central Pacific area must be closely coordinated to assure maximum effectiveness. It was by far better to have a single hand guiding the plan and maintaining control. He also felt he should be the man, but he was not in the position to force the issue.

He was beholden to Admiral King. King had gone to bat for him early in February at the Casablanca Conference. The British were adamant against any further increase in arms and men to the Pacific on the grounds it would reduce the impact of operations in Europe. They insisted that Europe was, and should remain until it was secured, the primary concern of the United States.

General George Marshall, with Admiral King at his side, assured the British that all new developments in the Pacific would be carried out with resources already assigned. The fact that Nimitz had requested and was in the process of receiving an entire fleet of ships and personnel to man them was by a prior commitment and this enabled Marshall to keep his promise. It also proved to be the saving factor in the Pacific. Nimitz had won a private victory and King had supported his plan. He could not ask for more.

Nimitz knew what his job was. He would pursue westward from Pearl Harbor with his best leadership and his hard-hitting warships, new and old. Who commanded the Fifth Fleet was entirely in Chester Nimitz's hands.

The Fifth Fleet was large and would grow even larger through the next few months — to six heavy and five light carriers, eight escort carriers, five new and seven old battleships, twenty-nine transports and cargo vessels, and a large number of landing craft. Nimitz was proud of this fleet and was prepared to release his own chief of staff, Admiral Raymond A. Spruance, a man of proven ability and sharp intellect, to command it. One of the young officers commented when the assignment was made that Nimitz was ready to let Spruance go since now they walked and talked and thought alike.

The amphibious component of the fleet was given to Rear Admiral Richmond Kelly Turner and the Amphibian Corps of marines was under the command of Major General Holland M. Smith. The setup could not be better. Nimitz was at last prepared to finish the job he had started over a year ago.

Early one morning in April during the reevaluation period, Nimitz received a surprising communique — one that had been decrypted and translated from a Japanese dispatch. Commander Layton took the news. "It's our old friend Yamamoto," he said, as he read the dispatch: "The Commander-in-Chief of the Combined Fleet will inspect Ballale, Shortland, and Buin on April 18 ... 6 a.m. depart Rabaul in medium attack plane escorted by six fighters ... 8 a.m. arrive Ballale ..." Yamamoto's complete itinerary for the day followed.

Nimitz looked at Layton in disbelief and then turned to the maps on the wall. Halsey was near the area and could easily take on the famous admiral. "Do we try to get him?" he asked of Layton.

Layton assured him that next to the emperor, Yamamoto was probably the most important man in Japan.

Nimitz hesitated only long enough to call for a staff member to direct a message to Washington. This was something the president should be aware of. He didn't want an international incident as a result nor did he want to cause undue political problems at home. King sent a return wire authorizing affirmative action. Nimitz immediately put out an alert to Halsey.

Relaying the entire Yamamoto itinerary to Halsey, Nimitz added a personal note. "Good luck and good hunting." Admiral Nimitz knew this word would be of particular importance to Halsey since he had been with Doolittle when they bombed Tokyo almost two years before.

Intelligence knew that Yamamoto was invariably punctual and was confident that the plane carrying Yamamoto would appear on schedule. At exactly the right time sixteen P-38 Lightnings from Henderson Field on Guadalcanal took off and flew more than 400 miles over open water before they spotted two Japanese "Betty" bombers — one carrying the admiral. Six Zero fighters were acting as escorts.

When the Japanese bombers realized they were being chased they broke formation to escape. Instantly, two of the American fighters bore down on Yamamoto's plane, shot off the right wing, and sent the "Betty" plummeting to the ground. The second "Betty" carrying Yamamoto's staff was also destroyed, crashing in the sea. Incredibly, several of its passengers survived. Several days later Japanese searchers found Yamamoto's body deep in the jungle.

On Palm Sunday, April 18, a report came into the CinCPac headquarters: The mission had been accomplished. "Congratulations to you and Major Mitchell and his hunters. Sounds as though one of the ducks in their bag was a peacock."

It was not until late in May that Nimitz and his staff knew the details. A Japanese communique revealed the truth. "While directing general strategy on the front line in April of this year, engaged in combat with the enemy and met gallant death in a war plane." Yamamoto's ashes were being returned to Japan on the super battleship *Musashi*.

Everyone knew the significance of this historical event. The consequences would have been as great had the Japanese forces intercepted Nimitz on one of his island hopping inspections. A dark and sustaining cloud hovered over Japan from that day.

Chester Nimitz had a personal philosophy about women and war. He never liked to have women in the war zone. He had repeatedly refused to have them come over from the states either as entertainers or as wives. When requests came for women to serve at Pearl Harbor he refused without an explanation. He only stated that when it was safe for women he would let them know. It was therefore not to his liking when he received a special request from the president of the United States.

"Dear Chester,
    Eleanor has decided she's got to come to the Pacific. I don't approve of the visit. If you want to turn her down, go ahead and do so."

The letter went on to state that Mrs. Roosevelt's main purpose for visiting was to represent the Red Cross and visit the sick and wounded.

Nimitz was stuck. He couldn't very well refuse the First Lady of the land and get by with it. He gave up and dutifully invited Mrs. Roosevelt with as much graciousness as he could muster.

Therefore, in August, under a heavy blanket of secrecy Mrs. Roosevelt landed at Pearl Harbor. Fortunately, an army general, Walter O. Ryan, who was in command at Hickam Field, arranged for the first breakfast for the First Lady to be at his home. He invited all the local senior officers and Admiral Nimitz. This gave Nimitz a little warming up time. That evening Mrs. Roosevelt dined at Admiral Nimitz's quarters, the Makalapa.

Chatting with her over dinner Admiral Nimitz resumed his courteous ways both as a gentleman and as a host. He was greatly impressed by Eleanor's seriousness and her dedication to the individual men in the wards. Soon they began exchanging jokes and Nimitz felt much more relaxed, pleased that she had as much a sense of humor as he did. He gave her a few of his Texas tales he had cleaned up and she countered with some funny incidents involving her and Franklin that few people had heard. The next day, Mrs. Roosevelt flew to the headquarters in Noumea and Admiral Halsey entertained her. When she returned to Hawaii Nimitz was by now pleased to show her around the island in his personal dark-blue admiral's barge.

The crew, knowing the First Lady was to come aboard, gave the barge their finest spit and polish, even revarnishing the deck for the occasion. Not realizing what she was doing, Mrs. Roosevelt came on board in high heel shoes and scraped the new varnish! Nimitz deliberately kept her mind and eyes on the scenes of the island when he noticed the crew members grimace at the damage to their beautiful handiwork.

Her good-will tour to the hospital proved to be a morale builder, and the public relations that had been created impressed Nimitz. As he escorted her to the plane he was a different man than he had been when she had arrived. She had made high marks with him.

Nimitz returned to his headquarters only to face a growing confrontation between his new commanders of the Fifth Fleet and the ground force generals.

Galvanic was the code name given the 1943-44 offensive move westward to the Gilbert and Marshall Islands. The Fifth Fleet had been organized and the orders given. The orders, however, were confusing to Admiral Turner of the navy and General H. M. Smith of the marines. They were cheek to jowl about what the orders really meant. Turner insisted that while the troops were on his ships and in his landing craft they were under his command. This applied to amphibious training and rehearsals as well as to the actual assault. Army Lieutenant General Richardson reminded Nimitz that he was in charge of training all soldiers in the Pacific, and he had been given control of the 27th Division right through the invasion. "Howling Mad" Smith was howling even louder than usual. His division of marines had been left in New Zealand because the army was being given the invasion responsibility. The argument grew loud and heated. Finally, Richardson appealed to Nimitz for a ruling on the command. Nimitz quickly responded: "All troops assigned to Operation *Galvanic* would be under the command of Smith."

This caused much discontent among the army personnel, so much so that Richardson appealed his case to General Marshall in Washington. Nimitz's command held firm and the operations went forward. The matter of interservice relations were strained even more and throughout the Pacific campaigns, constant attention had to be given to the assignments of the growing numbers of troops. It was a problem until the end of the war.

When Nimitz assumed command at Pearl Harbor in 1942, he had forty-five people under him at CinCPac headquarters. At the end of the hostilities this number had increased into the thousands and his entire Pacific command had grown to over 2,100,000 men.

In the next three months of 1943 the Fifth Fleet concentrated on the central Pacific operation and with the Allied forces of the navy, marines, and army, coordinating efforts for the Tarawa, Makin, and Gilbert Islands phase. The lessons learned proved invaluable, hard and costly though they were. Proper island fighting had to be studied and developed. Tarawa was one of the islands the Japanese had fortified in what was to be their classic way with seawalls of tough, green, coconut logs followed by a labyrinth of underground caves and structures for gun emplacements and shelter for troops. This kind of defensive bastion, with protective reefs, receding tides, and strong headwinds made the operation even more formidable. Advancement on Tarawa was slow and the losses were greater than any com-

ADMIRAL OF THE HILLS

ADMIRAL NIMITZ attends picnic at "Nimitz Beach" at Honolulu, September 1944. An example of the admiral's policy was associating with men at all levels.
— *Official U.S. Navy photo.*
Courtesy Admiral Nimitz State Historical Park

mander would have imagined. However, on the nights of November 22 and 23 the Japanese had been moved back and ultimately surrounded. The enemy pockets were reduced and more often than not the Japanese troops died rather than surrender. Ultimate victory came, but at a cost of more than 6,000 dead on one square mile of coral sand.

At the end of the second year in the Pacific Chester Nimitz could now see the end in sight. He and Admiral King had agreed upon the direction to be taken and it was now a matter of time, energy, materiel, and manpower. Nimitz's job increasingly became one of assigning personnel and for this he had no equal.

He had a way of surrounding himself with the most able in the navy. He knew what to look for relative to each particular job and responsibility. He became as adept at strategic selection and assignment of personnel as he was of combat operations.

Because of the tremendous difficulty of the engagement at Tarawa, Nimitz decided to fly over and take a personal look. Only two days after the massive invasion he took off despite the forewarnings of Admiral Spruance. Spruance suggested to Nimitz that he postpone his landing at Tarawa until the cleanup process had been completed. The heavy toll of men and the destruction was everywhere evident on the island, but Nimitz ignored the objections and met Spruance and General Julian Smith for an onsight inspection. Bodies and parts of bodies were strewn everywhere — sometimes singly, but more often in heaps. Nimitz was aghast. He remarked, "It's the first time I've smelled death." For the first time the admiral was aware of the extent to which the Japanese had gone to defend the island. He was deeply moved by the stench of death, the extent of sacrifice made by the Allied forces, and the weary appearance of the men who were left to bury the dead.

As Nimitz returned to Pearl Harbor he learned that the Americans had now acquired Abemama, another island in the Gilberts. An airstrip could be established there without difficulty.

The next day the restless admiral went aboard a new cruiser docked in the harbor and stayed on its deck while it began its departure to sea. A man in a small dingy saw the admiral go aboard and when he was out a short ways flashed a signal to the large ship from his tiny craft, "I'll not shoot until I see the whites of your eyes." To that the admiral signaled back, "Try not to kill us all with one shot."

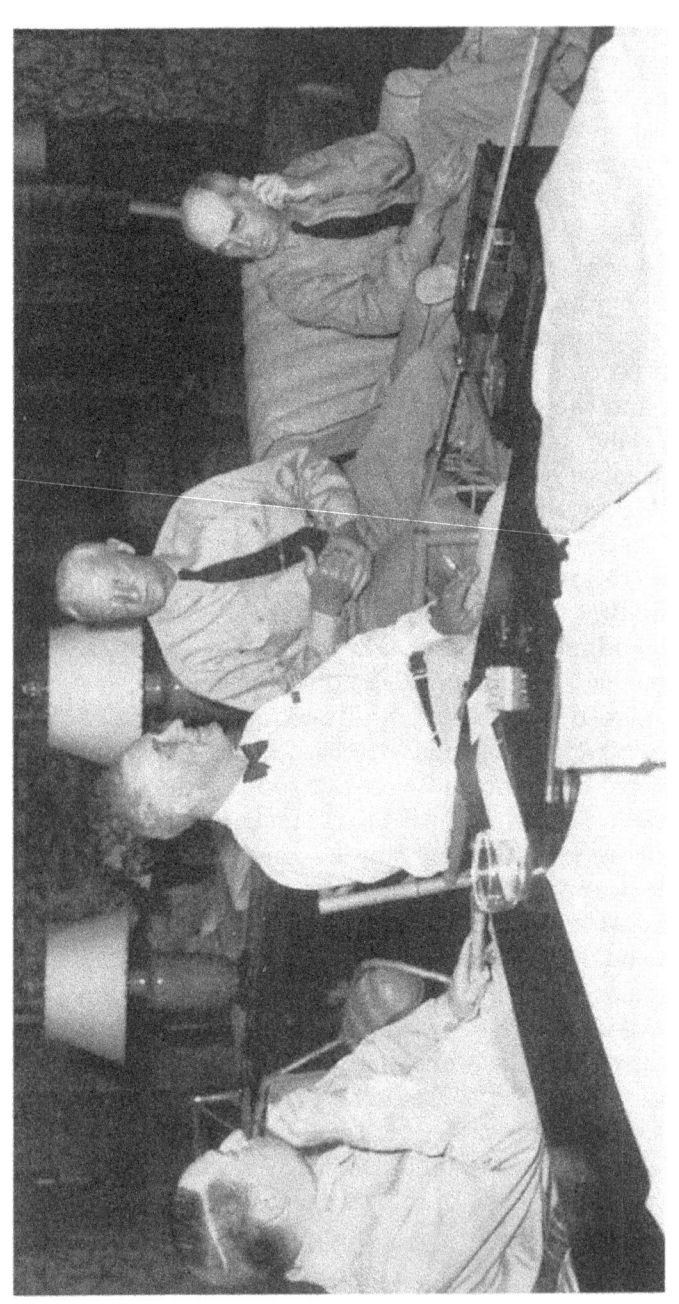

ADMIRAL NIMITZ AND General MacArthur meet with President Roosevelt during a trek to the war zone. Admiral William D. Leahy is shown at the right. — *Official U.S. Navy photo. Courtesy Admiral Nimitz State Historical Park*

---- 13 ----

1944

In the midst of planning for the second phase of penetration in the Gilbert and Marshall Islands, Admiral Nimitz decided to throw a Texas-size picnic. It was to be held at Moana Park in Honolulu on a Sunday afternoon. There was barbecue, beans, and cornbread. General Richardson and his army came and Admiral Nimitz and his navy. In all 40,000 army and navy men from Texas pitched horseshoes, told stories, and ate, drank, and made merry. A jukebox was rigged up in one corner of the park as new tunes from the states blared out for all the community to hear. "That Old Black Magic," and "I Left My Heart At The Stage Door Canteen" were two early favorites. One that the soldiers particularly liked was "Praise the Lord and Pass the Ammunition." The sailors and air force boys preferred "Coming in on a Wing and a Prayer." Even though it was January, they all liked and still listened to Bing Crosby sing "White Christmas."

In the middle of the afternoon Admiral Nimitz mounted a low, handmade podium and spoke to the crowd. It was a speech to be remembered by all Texans....

FRIENDS OF TEXANS AND FELLOW TEXANS —

Today we are thousands of miles away from the Great State we are proud to call Home. This gathering proves again that the ties that bind Texans together can be stretched a long way but cannot be broken. It shows you can take a man out of Texas, but you can't take Texas out of the man.

Texas is a state whose size is exceeded only by its importance. Texans take great pride in their heritage of brave traditions, in the geographic dimensions of their state, in its rich resources, in the great natural beauties of its broad terrain, and in the varied accomplishments of its citizens. Was it not a Texan — Al Dexter — who authored the song "Pistol Packin' Momma," now sweeping the country and destined to be sung all over the world? And did not our Army pay tribute to the tough and efficient fighting qualities of our Texas Rangers when they applied the name *RANGERS* to their super-soldiers — men who are readied for combat in special training and hardening courses.

There are, of course, many stories of the exploits of Texas Rangers, but the one I like best is one probably known to many of you. The mayor and sheriff of a Texas community asked for the help of a detachment of Rangers to suppress a riot then in progress. When the train bearing the expected detachment arrived a lone Ranger got off. To the sheriff's question, "Where is the detachment?" the

Ranger replied: "I'm it. Your wire specified only one riot."

But today we can add to the things of which we are proud, the splendid record of valor and achievement being won by the Sons of Texas on battlefields in all theatres of war. There are more than half a million native sons of Texas in the armed forces. A growing number of native daughters are represented in the auxiliary services, and a Texas woman is at the head of the Women's Auxiliary Corps of the Army. Furthermore, it is a Texas woman who conceived and organized this Roundup which so many of us are enjoying today. I take this opportunity to pay tribute to Miss Elizabeth Wright of Corpus Christi and Honolulu — a native Texan and a person of imagination and energy. On behalf of the Texans and their friends here assembled, I thank Miss Wright for making this party possible.

There are 400,000 native Texans in the Army, Texas has 95,000 of her sons in the Navy, 20,000 in the Marine Corps, and 2,500 in the Coast Guard. These men have distinguished themselves as units and as individuals.

The 36th Division is making a brilliant record in Italy. Recent press dispatches indicate the Germans believe the Texans composing this Division are some kind of a secret weapon. A German prisoner recently taken was quoted as saying they now were fighting "tough, wild men from Texas, very skilled in field craft." These men are alleged to be over ten feet tall and to swing a 75 millimeter gun from each hip. The 29th Seabee

Battalion, assigned to the Pacific Theatre, is predominantly composed of Texans and has been designed the Lone Star Battalion. They are making a splendid record in this theatre. It is rumored they contemplated building a tunnel under the Pacific to Tokyo in order to get closer to the shooting.

The first beachhead on New Britain Island was established by an assault force of Texans carrying the Lone Star Flag into battle with the Sixth Army under General Douglas MacArthur. This force was an outfit of dismounted cavalry from around Dallas and Fort Worth. How much more they might have accomplished had they had their horses under them is hard to tell. They might even be in the outskirts of Tokyo now.

The individual men to whom recognition has come for valor in action are legion. The most recent of these was Marine Lieutenant William D. Hawkins of El Paso, who led attack after attack against enemy machine gun positions at Tarawa and fought dauntlessly and furiously in spite of three wounds until finally he was killed in action. In his fighting spirit, in the fighting spirit of other Texans who have fallen on the field of battle, we take solemn pride. More than two thousand Texans have given their lives in the defense of our nation's cherished freedom. Their names will be forever enshrined in the hearts and minds of Texans, along with other earlier heroes of the republic.

A little more than a hundred years ago another Hawkins was playing a colorful part in Texas history. He was Commodore Charles E. Hawkins, first to command the Texas

Navy. Not many people realize that Texas once had a Navy of her own; that many of the pioneers were seafaring people, and that victories won at sea helped in shaping Texas destiny.

Most of the early settlers came by way of sea, embarking at Mobile and New Orleans. Because of their innocence, or because of a certain love of independence, they entered through whatever ports on the Gulf seemed most expedient.

The ports of entry which Mexico attempted to establish for the collection of customs duties were an early cause of friction which contributed to the Texas Revolution. And during the Revolution, the tiny Texas Navy, built around three ships of war under Commodore Hawkins was able to establish control of the Gulf of Mexico. These ships were the *Independence*, the *Invincible*, and the *Brutus*. With them Hawkins controlled the sea approaches to Texas, blocked reinforcements to Santa Anna and contributed in its long overland march to the Alamo, Goliad, and San Jacinto Battle of 1836. So it was that Texas established a Naval tradition to stand alongside the brilliant military record achieved on land.

At about the same time these restless men and women — mostly from the South — were migrating to Texas; the missionary movement from New England to these islands was underway. It is interesting to speculate on what might have happened had these sturdy, energetic, far-seeing men of religion gone to Texas instead of to Oahu. The annexation business might have been reversed and Texas, instead of joining the USA might have absorbed the rest of the Union. Then, Texas though still bounded on the south by Mexico and its Gulf would not have the rest of the country lying about it.

In reviewing our military achievements in this war, we should not slight the active and enthusiastic support of Texans left at home. You will recall that Texas citizens volunteered to buy enough war bonds to replace the cruiser *Houston* and oversubscribed their quota to such an extent that enough was left over to pay for the carrier *San Jacinto*. On this occasion the Governor of Texas assured the President that Texas would not declare a separate peace, but he could not guarantee that Texans would stop fighting at the end of the war. It is very comforting to know that our friends and relatives in Texas are fighting the battle of the homefront so valiantly and to such good purpose.

I notice that many of you here today are wearing the uniform of your country. I am well aware that many of you in civilian clothes are engaged in important defense work in these islands and I'm sure that all of you are helping to prosecute the war. As Texans I know each of you is devoted to our cause and determined to give your best until we accomplish the long hard job necessary to bring about the unconditional surrender of Japan. I say it will be a hard job because if there's one place bigger than Texas it's the Pacific Ocean. But all of us and hundreds of thousands of other Americans along with our allies, will roam these broad open spaces of the Pacific until our treacherous enemy is roped, tied, and properly branded so that our descendants may always recognize his true character. I hope all here may attend that roundup.

Now more than ever, the eyes of Texas are upon you. I am sure the deeds of her sons and daughters in future months will measure up to the high mark already made; indeed, that this record will be surpassed, and that you will not be so very much older before you will be able to march triumphantly back to Houston, to San Antonio — to Austin — Abilene and Clarendon, Fredericksburg, Kerrville — or wherever your home may be in Texas, and there receive the well-earned praise of the grateful citizens of Texas and of your country and there await the call for the next Roundup.

The crowd roared its applause in Texas fashion, as army, navy, and air force caps filled the air.

Admiral Nimitz was the most popular man at the picnic. He played with the men, talked with them, and signed his autograph for everyone interested. When the press wrote it up, Nimitz got the credit for "doing right" by the boys on the base. In every way the afternoon was declared a success.

That night, however, the Honolulu police reported they had never witnessed such an affair. The sanitation department agreed. Never had they had such a massive cleanup job. Even Admiral Nimitz admitted it was the worst destruction he had seen since Kwajalein was invaded.

Overall, those days would have never been construed as fun and games. When the picnic was going on the major portion of the admiral's "boys" were on the high seas, striking heavily at the Marshall Islands. By then the men were better trained for island combat. During the first week of February, Roi, Namur, and Kwajalein were declared secure and the fleet was moving northward and westward in the Marshalls with Eniwetok as their next target.

As soon as Eniwetok was taken in the middle of February, the Joint Chiefs of Staff called a high level conference in Washington, summoning Nimitz and MacArthur.

As usual MacArthur chose to decline and begged off, insisting that he could not in good faith leave his command. He sent a representative as was his custom. Nimitz, however, obeyed the orders and made plans to fly to Washington.

The Washington conference was to complete the strategy for the Mariana invasion. While Admiral Nimitz was there Mrs. Nimitz and daughter, Mary, came to the Capitol to join him. With an office and a secretary assigned to him, he felt like he was back on shore duty. At the Navy Department, the Waves and women marines had taken over. They were hard workers and were very visible... as well as attractive. It was not secret that all top officers assigned to help Nimitz while in residence were female. They were hoping the exposure to their efficiency and intellectual ability would persuade him to allow assignments of women to the South Pacific. Contrary to what they hoped would happen, Chester Nimitz retained his old-fashioned ways and could never get over the young women snapping to attention and saluting as he walked by. Though he was grateful for their help he nevertheless would not relent and allow female military personnel to come to the war front. This attitude continued as long as he was in command.

Before Nimitz returned to Pearl Harbor he had a visit with President Roosevelt. The president looked worn and ill and not as mentally alert as Nimitz had remembered leaving him in 1942. From the course of the conversation, Nimitz knew that the president was not up to tackling the heavy details of planning in the Pacific. Nimitz therefore made as light of the meeting as possible. He told the president a few jokes and produced many laughs. Nimitz felt the best thing to do was to leave in an atmosphere of friendship and good will.

To Nimitz's surprise when he returned to Pearl Harbor there was a radio message waiting for him from General MacArthur. It read: "I have long had it in my mind to extend to you the hospitality of this area. The close coordination of our respective commands would be greatly furthered I am sure by our personal conference. I would be delighted therefore if when you are able you would come to Brisbane as my guest. I can assure you of a warm welcome."

The ice had been broken. Repeatedly Nimitz had tried to get MacArthur to a meeting. He continually and constantly refused. Now here he was taking the initiative. Nimitz also knew the reason. MacArthur was disturbed and fearful that part of his command might be turned over to naval operations. The discussion of this had been paramount while in Washington, but the Joint Chiefs had decided to leave the boundaries as they were. They were aware MacArthur would not take lightly to any lessening of his authority. They also knew that had MacArthur had his way, all of the invasions up the ladder to the Japanese mainland would have been under his command. Those in Washington were very much aware of this and knew they had to play the game carefully.

Nimitz, however, held no grudge even though he had every right to. At one time MacArthur had 221 ships immobilized off the shores of Leyte simply because he wanted to maintain control, a situation Nimitz felt untenable and a poor waste of power in any man's language. He had a job to do and he realized close coordination of their commands would facilitate the progress of the war and bring peace that much sooner. Nimitz swallowed his pride and sent a return message in answer to MacArthur's invitation: "Your very kind invitation, which is greatly appreciated, was awaiting me on my return from Washington this morning. It will give me much pleasure to avail myself of your hospitality in the near future. I am certain that our personal conference will insure closest cooperation in the coming campaign. Within the next few days I shall acquaint you with the time it will be feasible to leave here."

Due to the delicate situation Nimitz took great pains in preparing for his visit with MacArthur. He ordered a huge bouquet of orchids for Mrs. MacArthur and clothes and candy for the general's young son, both of whom were in residence in Brisbane. In less than ten days Nimitz was on his way.

On his arrival MacArthur's aide conveyed to Nimitz an invitation to a banquet to be held later that evening at the hotel. Nimitz and his aide, Hal Lamar, accepted but insisted on stopping by MacArthur's penthouse suite prior to the dinner.

The diplomacy proved successful. The general and Mrs. MacArthur were greatly pleased with the display of exotic orchids and called the son from his bedroom to receive his gifts.

At the conference the next day the admiral was as formal as the general, each wanting to maintain arms length, since so much turf was at stake. However, the encounter proved to be worthwhile. The meetings went well. The hospitality was cordial and the decision on strategy amiable, with one exception. As Nimitz was about to leave a small matter of alternative planning came up. The Joint Chiefs of Staff had requested of both men alternative plans for moving faster and along shorter routes to the Luzon-Formosa-China triangle. MacArthur took this as personal criticism and would have no part of it. He blew his composure and insinuated that the "gentlemen" in Washington — away from the scene and the whistle of bullets — had no business trying to tell him what to do. Besides he said he had a commitment. He was going back to the Philippines as a sacred obligation whether they liked it or not. It did not matter whether it was logical or not.

Nimitz was equal to the situation and countered with a defense of the "gentlemen" in Washington who were men just like himself trying to do a job and were doing it rather well.

MacArthur's single line of attack through the Philippines would have to shift and include the leap to the Marianas with full naval armada.

Despite this difference of opinion, Nimitz enjoyed his visit with MacArthur. He realized he had met with a colorful man, full of complex moods and contrasts of temperament. Either those who met MacArthur admired him or were turned completely off by him. They either felt he was brilliant, or they despised his arrogance. There usually was not any middle ground. Nimitz respected his intelligence and was amused by his pompous attempt to draw attention to himself. Personally, MacArthur didn't appeal to Nimitz as a potential friend, but he respected his ability as a military leader.

After the April attack on some of the islands in the Carolines and the invasion of Biak in New Guinea in May the entire naval strategy concentrated all efforts on the islands in the Marianas. Even MacArthur, who was adamantly opposed the first time the plan was discussed, concurred this time. The two-pronged attack led by MacArthur's forces coming up from New Guinea and Nimitz's navy crossing the Central Pacific was now in full force. No matter which was to be the main force in the assault on the Japanese mainland everything now pointed toward Tokyo.

Attacks on Saipan, Guam, and Tinian were ordered to begin on June 12, only a week after the Normandy invasion in Europe. It proved to be a decisive campaign, very damaging to the Japanese. Their defenses included the usual island artillery that was well camouflaged, but their effectiveness had been lost. The Americans were now trained to combat mortar emplacements, pillboxes, and machine-gun nests far more efficiently due to the costly lessons learned in earlier campaigns. Yet the Japanese soldiers hung on to the bitter end. On July 9, Saipan was taken and by August 1 Tinian was established as an American naval base. August 10 Guam had surrendered and was made secure for support troops to begin moving in.

In the midst of all this heavy naval and land fighting, President Roosevelt decided to pay a call on Pearl Harbor. Some say since it was an election year it was a grandstand play, but the fact was that once again MacArthur and Nimitz were at odds concerning strategy. They had shifted from the single line of attack to the dual line, but MacArthur could not be moved from his rigid determination to first take Luzon, then the other Philippine islands, recapture the Netherlands East Indies and then move up to Japan from the south. Nimitz and King wanted to continue their original plans to move due west to the Carolines, then to the central Philippines, Iwo Jima, Okinawa, and then to Japan. Only the commander-in-chief himself could make the final decision upon his arrival at Pearl Harbor, as to the naval involvement.

The plans for the president's visit were thorough. Secret Service agents came in advance and prepared his headquarters and residence on Diamond Head.

Nimitz sent a special invitation to MacArthur. MacArthur declined, insisting that he was too busy. King then issued MacArthur an invitation. Again MacArthur declined, insisting that he was just too involved in his campaign to take time off. Next, General Marshall ordered him to Honolulu. Reluctantly, and miffed that he should have been called away from what he considered his first priority, MacArthur arrived at last with five members of his staff.

True to MacArthur's flamboyant, dramatic flair, he arrived just about an hour before the presidential cruiser docked. He declined to be a part of the welcoming committee and went straight to General Richardson's home where he was staying. Nimitz proceeded with due and proper protocol. All naval personnel were ordered to wear white uniforms, all mail was stopped, and security was at its maximum. With much pomp and flourish the welcoming contingent boarded the cruiser to greet their president. Immediately the presidential flag was hoisted and the crew of every ship lined the rails to salute and pay tribute to their leader.

Roosevelt politely accepted the military honor and then quizzically asked, "Where is MacArthur?" No sooner were the words out than sirens, whistles, cheering, and the roar of a motorcycle escort advanced to the pier. Out stepped MacArthur dressed in a pair of khakis, a brown leather jacket, a Filipino field marshal's cap, and smoking a corncob pipe. A cry sounded from the crowd gathered at the pier to celebrate this high-level occasion. MacArthur turned as he walked up the gangplank, acknowledged the cheering crowd, then proceeded to greet the president. He had upstaged everyone, his commander-in-chief included.

The president, not unfamiliar with MacArthur's dramatics, asked him as he shook his hand, "Douglas, why don't you wear the right kind of clothes when you come to see us?" No doubt Nimitz caught himself smiling inwardly under his stiff white uniform at the obvious contrast as pictures of this historic event would preserve for years the drama of the moment. Regardless of what the historians might say in years to come, it was a moment to remember. MacArthur endured the picture taking, but told his aide as he returned to his quarters that it was a bunch of political tomfoolery and that he was humiliated to be a part of such shenanigans.

The truth of the matter was that MacArthur had political aspirations himself, having allowed his name to be entered in the Republican primaries opposing Wendell Willkie and Thomas E. Dewey.

The meeting itself went about as Nimitz had planned. It was a two-man show. "Douglas" and "Franklin" did the conferring. Nimitz did the listening. MacArthur was so fearful of losing his coveted plan to the more direct and expeditious one of Nimitz and King that he was often insinuating, rude, and wrong. Nimitz felt he was childish in some of his overtures of superiority both to strategizing and evaluating; but Nimitz, being the host, allowed him to get by with it. He felt Roosevelt would have to be trusted to judge for himself, and since it was obvious from the total situation the two really had little reason for personal friendship between them, Nimitz felt the facts would eventually speak for themselves.

Besides the problems of the formal conference with the president and MacArthur, Nimitz had other things to think about. He was having Roosevelt at Makalapa for lunch the next day and the Secret Service men had ordered the house virtually rebuilt. There were doors to be enlarged and rehung, the bathroom had to be rebuilt for the president's wheelchair, the back of the house opened for a private entrance and given a new paint job. On the day before the luncheon, five hundred Seabees completely restructured the house and by the time the president arrived no one could have told it had not been that way all along. The paint was even dry — through the use of a blow torch.

As the conference ended with much fanfare of picture taking and press conferences, no one was exactly sure who won the day. MacArthur certainly felt he did, since he reported to Richardson as he took off for Brisbane, "We've sold it!"

Actually, the two men, Nimitz and MacArthur, reassured the president that they were now in agreement and that the next major assault would be on Leyte with logistical support from the Pacific fleet.

As final plans were drawn up to attack the Philippines, Halsey, Spruance, and the "dirty trick department" cut a broad swath across the archipelago of the Pacific islands attacking aggressively wherever they could. First it was Ulithi, then Peleliu, and many of the lesser islands. Reconnaisance was made by air for many of the future invasion sites such as Iwo Jima and Okinawa. Halsey, in order to deceive the enemy, steamed toward Luzon, but all the while was sending planes to the island of Formosa, destroying bases, airfields, shipping, and industry. By this time the Japanese came out in full force with some change in tactics and the nature of their attacks. The results were damaging to the Japanese, but they were soon to let loose the devastating "kamikaze" program that was to be a peril to the navy till the end of the war. "Kamikaze" would take admirals and common sailors to the utmost of skill, courage, fortitude, and tenacity to subdue.

In the meantime, the raids against the Carolines cleared the way for MacArthur's invasion of the Philippines. The initial landing at Tacloban, capital of Leyte, was virtually unopposed.

This was the day MacArthur had been waiting for. It was the day he had promised would come. On October 20, a broadcast was made: "People of the Philippines! I have returned. By the grace of Almighty God, our forces stand on Philippine soil . . . Rally to me! Strike at every favorable opportunity, for your home and your heart, strike!"

A separate great moment in history added to the American progress. The battle of Leyte Gulf climaxed the greatest naval build-up in history.

Nimitz took the news with mixed emotion. He was grateful for the return, but he couldn't help agreeing with the sailor he overheard saying, "By the grace of God and with a few marines, General MacArthur retook the Philippines." One more time MacArthur was capturing the headlines while the navy and the marines fought to the bone.

In September, 1944 President Roosevelt and Prime Minister Winston Churchill met in Quebec for their seventh major conference since the start of World War II. Admiral King was invited to join them. The men were seeing the light at the end of a long tunnel and were confident of winning the war.

It was clear at this point that the war in the Pacific, however, had been largely an American affair and suddenly Britain was offering to come in. Churchill explained, "The time had now come for the liberation of Asia, and I was determined that we should play our full and equal part in it."

The official reaction to the statement was reserved and designed not to offend the prime minister, but off-the-record comments in some cases were less than favorable. Churchill's further insistence did not help the situation.

"What I feared most at this stage of the game," he went on to say, "was that the United States would say in later years: 'We came to your help in Europe and you left us alone to finish off Japan.'" Therefore, Churchill proposed sending part of the British fleet to the Pacific to serve under the American command — which in this case was Nimitz.

Without thinking the matter through, or consulting others, Roosevelt replied magnanimously, "I should like to see the British fleet whenever and wherever possible."

No matter what the reaction from the leaders in the Pacific was, the die was cast. On the other hand the magnanimous gesture immediately turned sour. The logistics for the merger were wrong. Admiral King opposed the possibility because he believed the British ships would be unable to stay at sea for long periods of time. He also knew the United States now had the ability to finish the job alone.

Later in the year Admiral Nimitz received a barrage of messages from London and Sydney signaling the imminent arrival of Admiral Sir Bruce Frazer, the commander-in-chief of the British Pacific fleet. He inserted a memo to Admiral King in Washington: "I do not need Paul Revere (with his three lanterns) to tell me the British are coming."

When Admiral Frazer did arrive at Pearl Harbor Nimitz greeted him cordially and outlined his plans for the future involvement with his majesty's navy. Nimitz suggested that the British might be most helpful occupying themselves deep in the southwest Pacific, raiding Japanese oil installations on Sumatra. Naturally, this didn't set too well with

JAPANESE CARRIER bombed and torpedoed by navy planes October 24, 1944. — *Official U.S. Navy photo.*
Courtesy Admiral Nimitz State Historical Park

AIRFIELD IN THE Palau Islands, which was by-passed during World War II. The Japanese chiseled "Welcome Yankee" into the white coral. — *Official U.S. Navy photo.*
Courtesy Admiral Nimitz State Historical Park

the ambitious British, since they had far more glorious things in mind, mainly a significant role in the Okinawa operation. This gave Nimitz his out. He turned them over to Admiral Spruance to see if he could incorporate them in the planning.

Spruance was not anxious to try to infuse a different style of operational methods at Okinawa itself at this stage in the game. He suggested to them it would be helpful if the British force would serve as a shield to protect the fleet at Okinawa from attacks out of the Sakishima group of islands, down by Formosa.

The British complied without another word and did a splendid job. Even before the British entered the picture the Japanese were in trouble. The summer of 1944 found their homeland in jeopardy. The empire of their dreams was fast fading. Admiral Ohnishi, planner of the Pearl Harbor attack, said as he stood before twenty-four young pilots stationed at Mabalacat airfield near Manila, "The salvation of our country is now beyond the powers of the ministers of state, the general staff, and lowly commanders like myself. It can come only from spirited young men such as you. Thus on behalf of your hundred million countrymen, I ask of you this sacrifice, and pray for your success."

That was the beginning of *kamikaze*, a sign of quiet desperation. The Japanese knew the war was all but lost. Suicide missions sacrificially made were their only hope. It was a brave and costly move.

The very word *kamikaze* — "divine wind" — carried a connotation that went deep into Japanese spirituality. A source of divine hope that went beyond any human measure.

After much ceremony the first volunteers set out on their last mission, from which they would not return. The first attempt was successful. Hits were

ADMIRAL NIMITZ chats with Sir Bruce Frazer, admiral and commander of the British Pacific fleet on board the *Duke of York* in Guam Harbor, 1945.
— *Official U.S. Navy photo.*
Courtesy Admiral Nimitz State Historical Park

made on navy ships — the *Santee, Suwanee, Kalinin Bay, Sangamon* and *White Plains*. The cruiser *St. Louis* was sunk.

Nineteen forty-four was a year of disappointment for the Japanese with hope for victory becoming increasingly dim. The story was different for the Allied forces. Much time had passed since Doolittle's flight over the Japanese homeland in 1942. The die was now cast for the massive bombardments of the Japanese mainland. Everything in the Allied cause was gearing up for the finale, in Europe and in the Pacific.

In order to match the American commanders in rank with their allies, Congress established a new level of military commission for generals and admirals to be denoted by five stars. On December 19, 1944, four generals and three admirals were given this rank. The president made the appointment of Marshall, MacArthur, Eisenhower, and Arnold five-star generals, and Leahy, King, and Nimitz as Fleet Admirals.

It was a touching moment for Nimitz on the day he received his commission as Fleet Admiral. His sailor metalsmiths had a new collar insignia ready for the occasion. It was five stars designed in a circle and a fitting moment for one of Nimitz's puns, so he feigned bedazzlement and said, "For a second there I saw stars."

The year ended with Nimitz once again on his way to Leyte to counsel with MacArthur concerning the naval support for the imminent invasion of Luzon. The general was in a great frame of mind as he announced the end of heavy resistance of the Japanese on Leyte, but his countenance fell when he noticed Nimitz wearing his five-star collar insignia while he had none! Before nightfall MacArthur ordered his aides to prepare such an insignia for him to wear the next morning. They were ready for him — filed from Filipino ten-cent pieces!

214 ADMIRAL OF THE HILLS

PRESIDENT HARRY S TRUMAN chats with ranking naval officers aboard the USS *Franklin D. Roosevelt* during fleet maneuvers off the Virginia Capes. — *Official U.S. Navy photo. Courtesy Admiral Nimitz State Historical Park*

---- 14 ----

1945

The new year brought both good and bad news. The good news was that Admiral Nimitz was moving his headquarters to Guam. The bad news was that MacArthur was still having trouble in the Philippines; the *kamikazes* were attacking regularly and destroying major ships and carriers; a typhoon struck capsizing three destroyers, seven other ships were severely damaged, 186 planes were blown overboard, and nearly 800 men and officers were lost. Nimitz's report to Washington stated it was the greatest loss in the Pacific without compensatory return since the battle of Savo Island.

Nimitz had been planning to move his headquarters to Guam for some time. Always defensive about the fact he had to stay at Pearl Harbor, due to staff records and secret documents, he was happy to get closer to the action. Moving to a forward area would take him a thousand miles closer to the fighting, but would take him out of the atmosphere of a bureaucratic setting. By now CinCPac had increased in size and number to a point that all attempts at informality were out of the question. It was a little Navy Department all its own. Secretly, Nimitz also wanted to be more a part of the risk as well as the strategy, as any navy man would. The fact that he was now a five-star Fleet Admiral meant even more security was given to him personally. This made Nimitz all the more anxious for a little breathing room and the chance to show that being the highest didn't necessarily mean the least accessible. Nimitz wanted to be near the front. Headquarters at Guam would be more to his liking.

When he arrived at Guam, Nimitz's major focus turned to Iwo Jima and Okinawa. Iwo was needed as a base from which to operate, especially as a fighter base and for an emergency landing for B-29 bombers returning from Japan.

Iwo Jima was as one pilot noted, "the most unpredictable target in the Pacific." Over half the time the ugly eight-mile-square island was covered with heavy clouds overhead and a fortress hiding Japanese underground. An unbelievable maze of tunnels and interweaving networks of underground bunkers, ridges, gorges, and ledges awaited the unprepared Americans. Entire hills had been hollowed out to hide hundreds of Japanese soldiers prepared to defend the island to the death. The situation was simply nothing the navy or marines had ever encountered or anticipated before.

Consequently the battle was one of the longest and hardest of the Pacific. It took the navy and the marines ten days of hard fighting to claim victory. The losses to both nations were monumental. Then finally when the marines raised the American flag, it was more than a perfunctory duty. It was in tribute to the tremendous sacrifice made in securing it. Joe Rosenthal, the Associated Press photographer, captured the dramatic scene in a picture that became the symbol of victory to all Americans.

Iwo was said to have been the bloodiest prize of the Pacific, but its value had neither been exaggerated or underestimated. Twelve days before the island was declared secure the first B-29 made an emergency landing there. In less than three weeks 108 P-51 Mustangs left from the Iwo Jima airstrip to escort a daylight B-29 attack on Tokyo. Before three months passed more than 850 B-29s had made emergency landings on the island, thus confirming the necessity for taking the island in the first place. No question that without this key base most of them would have been lost at sea.

The price of Iwo Jima was extraordinarily high. Out of 23,000 Japanese on the island only 1,083 were ever taken prisoner. For the American forces, some 6,821 marines and sailors lost their lives. It had been a fight of unprecedented fury and had to leave the concerned American military leaders in a quandary. To take such a tiny island at such a tremendous cost over a period of thirty-six days with the best of all available manpower, how much would it cost to take Japan? The question was formidable — a question which no one took lightly.

Secretary of Navy Forrestal (Secretary of the Navy Knox had died a few months earlier) witnessed the raising of the flag on Iwo Jima and returned to report firsthand the situation there. The select group in Guam who gathered to celebrate the victory had additional reason to celebrate. It was Chester Nimitz's sixtieth birthday — one which he would never forget.

Shortly after Forrestal left, Nimitz decided to return to Washington. En route he stopped at Pearl Harbor and San Francisco. Here he learned again what was typical of the news stories being published and circulated in the states. An editorial appeared in the *San Francisco Examiner* lauding the leadership of MacArthur. It said in declarative language that MacArthur was the only person smart enough to win the war, and that he was not losing men and equipment as other commanders were doing. Washington should let MacArthur take over the total command of the Pacific. The navy and marines did not have the leadership. It was obvious, the editorial stated, that the leadership they had was risking the lives of American boys unnecessarily.

This made Nimitz burning mad. It made the marines furious enough to storm the newspaper building demanding an apology. The apology never came, but Nimitz was now on guard to all attacks that would come his way criticizing his style of leadership and command against the strategies of "King" MacArthur.

Nimitz proceeded on to the White House to visit with President Roosevelt. The meeting saddened Nimitz a great deal. The president was visibly ill. His clothes draped like they might on a skeleton. He had difficulty talking and his hands shook noticeably. Nimitz had the distinct impression this would be the last time he would ever see Roosevelt. His mission accomplished — that of approval to follow his main line on to Okinawa — Nimitz returned to Pearl Harbor with new determination to end the fighting in the Pacific in '45 and while Roosevelt still lived. In spite of public sentiment in the states he had a war to take care of.

Naturally, Nimitz did not take the criticism lightly. Daily he received letters from mothers of sailors and marines accusing him of sending their sons into battle knowing they would not survive. Lamar tried to shield him from as many of the more irate letters as possible, but Nimitz felt he must respond as best he could, and especially to the most vicious. He was not the popular man in the Pacific that MacArthur appeared to be. Some were letters cursing him for being a poor leader and strategist and calling him all kinds of warmongering names.

Popularity didn't score with Nimitz. The human element did. No one likes to be called a murderer even when it is the line of duty. He reevaluated his own mind and placed himself in the shoes of those who really couldn't know the makeup of the war. He felt deeply distressed and did everything he could to soothe the troubled minds of those who thought he had acted wrongly and without regard to personal loss.

Chester wrote to Catherine daily of these disturbing feelings and one day confessed to her how deeply he grieved for each man, and he wished to God it had not had to be so — but for the life of him, he didn't see how he could have avoided it.

This was not the only problem weighing on Nimitz. The marine generals were on him again. The loss of marines had been enormous and Okinawa was now adding to the number. "Howling Mad" Smith was sent back to Pearl Harbor almost as a basket case over the tremendous loss sustained on Iwo Jima. General Vandegrift flew quickly to Guam requesting to visit his troops in Okinawa and judge for himself if something could be done to circumvent future losses. Nimitz refused to let him go.

Vandegrift was angered. He was in charge of his marines and he was going to Okinawa even though he tried to understand why Nimitz refused to allow him to go. Nimitz explained he wanted to go himself, but that fighting was so heavy and the risk so great that he could not have any high level interference at this point in the battle — even by himself.

Vandegrift attempted to reconcile his anger and

was surprised when Nimitz had a change of heart the next day and suggested that the two of them go to the front at Okinawa.

No one ever knew what changed Nimitz's mind; either word from Washington that no one could refuse a general from visiting his men or an "unusual change in circumstances" on the island, but the tour was made and Nimitz was given the benefit of the doubt.

Okinawa presented another problem for both the navy and the marines. It was one of the largest islands targeted for takeover by the Americans and had a topograpical feature generally associated with atolls. It was surrounded by coral reefs that made crossing tortuous and difficult. The Americans had learned something about coral reefs at Tarawa and were better prepared to cope with the problem.

The fighting on Okinawa proved erratic and surprising. All went well ahead of schedule the first few days. Out of the 60,000 men to land only twenty-eight had lost their lives by the end of the first day. The invasion went almost too smoothly but the effect was short lived. The Japanese resistance took a surprising turn.

The initial impression was deceiving. Lieutenant General Mitsuru Ushijima, the Japanese commander, had another plan — a plan he knew would be a lost cause for the Japanese, but would be almost as detrimental to hundreds of Americans.

He prepared defense lines in stages and was superbly equipped to wage a war of attrition. He had more weapons than any other Japanese commander had had in the entire Pacific war and over 80,000 men. He therefore made the fight a long and brutal one as the Americans slowly inched their way south through the Japanese fortresses hidden in caves and dugouts in the rough interior of Okinawa.

FLEET ADMIRAL NIMITZ shakes hands with his old friend, Governor Coke R. Stevenson, during a trip to Texas.
— *Official U.S. Navy photo.*
Courtesy Admiral Nimitz State Historical Park

NIMITZ INSPECTS the facilities of Photo Group Two at Agana, Guam, May 2, 1945.
— *Official U.S. Navy photo.*
Courtesy Admiral Nimitz State Historical Park

The Americans soon discovered the effectiveness of Ushijima's intricate and almost invulnerable defenses in the southern part of the island. It took nearly three months for the army, along with the Marines, to drive through the last of the defenses completely since they had to secure victory a little at a time.

The capture of Okinawa was slow. The ground operations almost bogged down and Nimitz insisted on speeding things up in order to release his supporting fleet, but the army had their own problems. Nimitz was losing a ship and a half a day, sunk or put out of action by heavy *kamikaze* attacks.

In spite of criticism from places high and low, Nimitz maintained his patient demeanor. He had no patience with the outcome of poorly executed tactics, but he knew that to be a true admiral, he had to make things work, regardless. He issued a statement at one of his few press conferences commending the army personnel and said that securing the island would have been far more costly and time consuming had amphibious landings behind the Japanese lines been attempted. He lauded the army's magnificent performance and then left it to the historians to determine the real cause of problems in the deadly Okinawa campaign. Admiral Nimitz listened to the questions: Why did the army adopt a slow course; and why were the marines not given full opportunity to carry out their style of leadership as they were trained to do? The answers were coming from war correspondents who enjoyed alarming the American public more than helping the combined heads of authority to do their job. Even some of Nimitz's own navy men were asking the same questions of him, inferring Nimitz to be wrong and bullheaded. It seemed everyone was having his doubts about the way Nimitz was handling the campaign. Nimitz held his course just the same and in the long run an overall confidence was maintained and the trust of his men prevailed. For Nimitz, personally, it was a grim and frightening time. His judgments and decisions were being tested by some of his strongest and most supportive men. As a result Nimitz felt they had to be replaced for harmony to prevail.

As the last gun was fired and the supporting ships slipped away from the shores of Okinawa, a count was made of this historical battle. Over 90,000 Japanese had died and some 11,000 were taken prisoner. For the Americans twenty-six naval vessels had been sunk and 368 damaged, many beyond repair. The U.S. forces lost 7,613 soldiers and marines, with nearly 39,000 wounded. Almost 5,000 sailors lost their lives and about the same number were wounded, mostly by *kamikaze* action.

On the other side of the ledger, the tremendous sacrifice bought for the Allies bases for a bombing campaign to be launched toward the mainland of Japan. More than that, it forced Japan and its leaders to face the inevitable truth — victory could never be theirs. The longer they held out the more costly it would be for their already sadly depleted forces. The "Rising Sun" was beginning to set.

In the midst of all the in-house fighting MacArthur had come up with another plan. His drive from New Guinea had not advanced as dramatically as he had expected and there was no question but Admiral Nimitz's forces were moving toward the mainland faster. MacArthur blamed it on restriction from Washington. His considerable talents were being wasted on secondary objectives, and thus again, the old argument for the establishment of a unified command under MacArthur was brought up.

MacArthur, understanding he had the president's full backing, sent a courier to Nimitz saying he would soon take over complete control of army forces under Nimitz, including the garrisons of island bases in the Pacific areas. This would break up Nimitz's unity of command which he termed "an unworkable shibboleth" and would make it impossible for any army troops in the future to serve under any admiral.

Nimitz's patience had taken all it was about to take. The quiet, stubborn, strong-willed man turned to the courier and expressed himself. In no way was he about to succumb to MacArthur's demands. Were he to do so would be to bow to MacArthur as a subordinate.

Nimitz realized, nonetheless, that the termination of the war was more important than the egos of two men or the petty conflicting commands of two branches of the armed forces. Knowing that MacArthur would never consent to come to him, he, therefore, invited himself to Manila to confer with MacArthur and see the war to its end, with some kind of mutual agreement.

On a one-to-one basis MacArthur could be reasonable and Nimitz could be persuaded. In the confidence both men were striving for the same ultimate goal, they spent two days working for a mutual meeting ground and strategy for the last approach to Japan by sea, air, and land.

Nimitz went back to Guam, tired but satisfied he had done all he knew to. It was his goal to assure victory as soon as possible with the least loss of life and with minimum damage to the relationship within the armed services. Nimitz realized his dream of a unified army and navy was further away than ever. Minds and loyalties were too sensitive. Each had to give up something in order for victory to be a reality. Nimitz felt he had done his share of backing off this time.

In the meantime, word came to CinCPac of the death of President Roosevelt. Nimitz was not surprised. Roosevelt had looked like death when he saw him only five weeks before. He sent his condolences to Mrs. Roosevelt and began to wonder what might transpire with Harry Truman as the new president.

He wasn't long in finding out. Back in February a young navy officer had brought Nimitz a top secret communique from King announcing the development of the atom bomb. Nimitz was aghast at the proportions of damage one single bomb could do and confessed to the officer as he attempted to comprehend the vast destructive capacity involved that "he was probably born a few years too soon."

Now in July Operation *Olympic* and Operation *Coronet* were approved by President Truman for execution in August. In the meantime, Nimitz was continuing his raids on the mainland of Japan, bombing cities while submarines and mine-bearing planes were pushing back Japanese attacks on the islands.

There was hope Japan would surrender before the new bomb had to be used. He consulted with Layton as to the possibility of Japan surrendering. Layton felt the *samurai* tradition was too imbedded in the Japanese psychology for them to surrender anytime soon. They were committed to victory, he said, even though it appeared hopeless.

Nimitz considered the atom bomb inhuman and immoral, and certainly unethical. In his mind it was not a legitimate means of warfare, but he agreed with what Layton was saying and the mind of the Japanese was a vital part of what he had to deal with. This was, of course, coupled by the fact that he did not want to sacrifice any more American lives.

On August 6, a B-29 set out from Tinian in the early hours of the morning carrying the first atom bomb. At exactly 8:15 Hiroshima felt the funnel of death spread out and heap destruction beyond any possible imagination. Unlike any other destructive weapon the atom bomb exploded about 1,900 feet above the ground causing a mushroom-shaped cloud of white smoke to rise upward to 295,000 feet. In less than fifteen minutes the "black rain" sent radioactive particles back to earth and enveloped the entire city in a holocaust of flames. In a twinkling of an eye over 70,000 inhabitants of the city never saw another sunrise.

The ultimatum set down at the Potsdam Conference was now reissued to the Japanese. The ultimatum had been formed by the three major powers, the United States, Britain, and China and had been previously issued in July. But Japan ignored it. It had stated that the Japanese government must surrender unconditionally; be stripped of all territorial possessions except the four home islands; and points of its mainland would be occupied until a peaceful and responsible government could be established.

Again the world waited. What was Japan thinking and why were they so stubborn, Nimitz wondered. Surely by now they had to know they could not win. They must certainly respond to reason.

Still no word came from the Japanese.

At 3:30 a.m. on August 9 another plane took off with an atom bomb. The target — Nagasaki!

The damage and destruction again were unbelievable and soon word was received at CinCPac from Admiral King that the Japanese were asking for a cease-fire, or as King stated, "The Japanese have capitulated."

For Nimitz the news brought the realization of a dream that would bring a new tomorrow — a tomorrow that had only been a vision for many brave men who had already made the supreme sacrifice for freedom.

Layton stood and watched Nimitz. He didn't jump up and down with joy as Halsey was reported to have done when he heard the news. Rather, Nimitz quietly sat down in his chair as a satisfied smile — one that came from an inner conviction — rippled across his face. He had known they must surrender. He was only relieved that they had done so before another bomb could bring added destruction.

Nimitz immediately ordered new tactics. To be sure no more *kamikazes* were in the air ready to deliver their last full measure of retaliation he stated, "Investigate and shoot down all snoopers — not vindictively but in a friendly sort of way." Then as an afterthought, he reminded all forces that they should conduct themselves as gentlemen, officers, and men.

Even at the last Nimitz was a gentleman.

While all the hoopla was being heard across the nation, President Truman announced over the radio that he had appointed General Douglas MacArthur Supreme Commander of the Allied Forces and directed him to arrange for the surrender ceremonies and the official signing of the documents of peace.

"That did it," stormed Nimitz. He was utterly disgusted, not so much for himself but for the brave men in the navy and marines who had taken the greatest brunt of the battles of the Pacific. It proved once again that MacArthur demanded and got the limelight. It seemed the whole world again focused on him implying that it was his forces that had been instrumental in winning the war against the Japanese.

Nimitz was indignant and said so to Admiral King. King immediately proposed to the president that if an army general was going to conduct the peace treaty it should be done on a naval vessel rather than on land. So it was, the concession was made and Admiral Bill Halsey's *Missouri* was chosen for the cremony. Halsey sent a special message to the Naval Academy Museum requesting the loan of the American flag that Commodore Matthew Calbraith Perry had flown when he entered Tokyo Bay in 1853, for this historic occasion. The request was granted.

The details of the signing were set up by MacArthur with the Japanese government. Two days before it took place, Nimitz made one last parting gesture toward MacArthur. He ordered his Seabees to fix a landing boat to look like an army version of an admiral's barge. He offered this to MacArthur as his transportation to the ceremony on the *Missouri*.

MacArthur took a look at it and claimed it was "too small — I want a large vessel, and a new one. A destroyer is the only thing that will do."

MacArthur got his destroyer, the *Nicholas*, but the question of whose flag was to fly over the masthead of the *Missouri* was still a touchy subject. Nimitz gave the entire problem to Commander Lamar saying he was the flag lieutenant. It was his problem and Lamar solved it as any fair-minded man would do. For the first time in naval history there were two five-star flags flown side by side.

The ceremony was brief but memorable on that second day of September 1945. The chaplain gave the invocation and the band played "The Star Spangled Banner." MacArthur spoke his unforgettable speech of peace and then invited the representatives of the Imperial Japanese Government to move forward and sign.

MacArthur asked Lieutenant General Jonathan Wainwright and General Sir Arthur Percival, both former prisoners of war, to stand behind him as he signed the historical document.

Admiral Chester Nimitz came forward and signed for the United States of America.

Nimitz was followed by those who signed for Great Britain, China, Russia, Australia, Canada, France, The Netherlands, and New Zealand.

When all had finished MacArthur again stepped forward for a last and final word, "Let us pray that peace be now restored to the world and that God will preserve it always."

The ceremony ended at 9:25, just as the sun broke through the clouds and a flight of 450 carrier aircraft along with several hundred army air force planes flew over.

Some could hear, perhaps, in that dramatic moment, the stirring words sung in sacred and somber times and now made even more sacred by sacrifice, the navy hymn:

> Eternal Father, strong to save,
> Whose arm hath bound the restless wave,
> Who bidst the mighty ocean deep
> Its own appointed limits keep;
> O hear us when we cry to thee
> For those in peril on the sea.

Nimitz retired to his quarters on the *Missouri* to write Catherine and the children about the historic occasion. He rejoined his comrades for lunch, and then took the plane back to Guam.

In less than a week Admiral Chester W. Nimitz was at the airstrip boarding a plane that would take him back to Pearl Harbor and on to San Francisco. It was a tender moment for him. He was tired, but exhilarated, saddened but fulfilled, happy but grieved. He was one of the ones who was going home.

He left Guam, never to return.

JAPANESE NAVAL dignitaries visit Fleet Admiral Nimitz at his home in Berkeley, California, January 25, 1959.
— *Official U.S. Navy photo.*
Courtesy Admiral Nimitz State Historical Park

5

NIMITZ

The Peacemaker

CHINESE AMBASSADOR, Dr. Wellington Koo, hands Fleet Admiral Nimitz the first piece of cake during a ceremony at the Chinese Embassy, Washington, D.C., March 8, 1947.
— *Official U.S. Navy photo.*
Courtesy Admiral Nimitz State Historical Park

MR. YKASAKI, vice consul of Japan, San Francisco, California, shakes hands with Fleet Admiral Nimitz at Treasure Island.
— *Official U.S. Navy photo.*
Courtesy Admiral Nimitz State Historical Park

---- 15 ----

Cheers

The war was over. Military personnel in the Pacific and in the Atlantic were preparing to come home. Families waited by their radios with uncontrolled exuberance for news of the return of their sons, their husbands, their brothers, and their fathers. The streets were filled with shouting people as the bottled up tensions of the entire nation were released in every hamlet and village. It was a time of national celebration.

It was also a time for the traditional heroes' welcome. General Dwight D. Eisenhower and General Jonathan M. Wainwright were receiving huge receptions in Washington and New York for their leadership in the war. Secretary of the Navy Forrestal felt the commander-in-chief of the Pacific deserved as much credit for victory as the army and was preparing a ticker-tape celebration early in October.

At first Nimitz was against such an elaborate project. When confronted with the fact that two major military figures had already received accolades from the government and citizenry alike and knowing that General Douglas MacArthur's welcome would soon be forthcoming, Nimitz agreed. He wanted honor to go to the navy and marines for all they had done and certainly he was the national figure who represented them.

To Nimitz's mind the naval efforts won the war in the Pacific and the people should be made aware of it. He was sure that future historians would support him in that because the facts were self-evident. Nimitz was prepared and anxious to make some statements to this effect and with them give his opinions on the role of the United States in the future.

According to Forrestal's planning, October 5, 1945, was designated as "Nimitz Day" in Washington. On that day Nimitz would address a joint session of Congress, be honored by a three-mile-long procession, and be decorated by President Harry S Truman. In addition the battleship *Missouri*, now being dressed up for the occasion, would carry Nimitz from Norfolk, Virginia, up the coast to New York, with the admiral's flag flying at the main as a fitting gesture of victory and honor.

Unfortunately this segment of the plan did not set well with the president. When he learned of the use of the *Missouri* in the proceedings, he vetoed it. He, himself, had designs on the *Missouri*, perhaps because of its historical role in the signing of the peace, but perhaps, too, because it was named for the president's home state. Whatever the reason he had in mind using it himself on the big Navy Day show in New York later in the month. He planned to utilize the *Missouri's* deck as a platform from which to broadcast the speech he planned to give on that day. It was obvious that the president was not going to allow any infringement on his status as commander-in-chief.

This rejection came as no surprise to Nimitz. He

suspected the president's preference about the navy was not as strong as for the army, but he did not voice his feelings. This was not the time for controversy. It was a time of good will.

On his way to Washington for the celebration, Nimitz stopped off in San Francisco. Not a stranger here, this city had hosted him and Admiral King for many of CominCH-CinCPac meetings during the Pacific campaign. Also, Catherine and Mary had lived and worked there during the war. Acting Mayor Dan Gallaher invited him to city hall for a special tribute.

There, before a large gathering the mayor presented Admiral Nimitz with the key to the city. When he did, Nimitz commented, "What wouldn't Yamamoto have given for this!"

The clamor of applause went up in spontaneous appreciation. Each city official and citizen of San Francisco felt the true impact of that statement. Being on the West Coast and vulnerable, as well as being the seat of many high level naval conferences during the war, it felt close to this steady, dependable, vigilant man of the sea.

The next morning the homecoming party, Admiral and Mrs. Nimitz, Commander Hal Lamar, and Rear Admiral Forrest Sherman, set down in Washington and the Fleet Admiral prepared for an exceptionally busy day. He and his party were driven immediately to the Capitol where he was to make his first major speech to the members of Congress and the people of the United States.

It was an awesome moment. Few people are ever invited to speak before the joint Houses of Congress. Generally the honor is reserved for those whom Congress not only wishes to recognize in a special way, but even more important, those to whom they wish to listen. This event was no excep-

NIMITZ RIDES with President Harry Truman down Pennsylvania Avenue in Washington during the return parade.
— *Official U.S. Navy photo.*
Courtesy Admiral Nimitz State Historical Park

NAVY WAVES March down Pennsylvania Avenue in Washington, D.C., During Nimitz parade in 1945.
— *Official U.S. Navy photo.*
Courtesy Admiral Nimitz State Historical Park

tion. Every member was in his place. The aisles were overflowing and the balcony packed.

Nimitz stood to talk. He had four main points to emphasize. In time they became the theme for all his postwar speeches. His belief in them was unshakeable.

He earnestly appealed to the gathered congressmen and senators for the maintenance of strong sea power, ready for use whenever required. Nimitz knew his history. America had never been ready for war. As a nation we had always responded to overt attacks without the proper arms or men adequately prepared to defend the nation. "Failing this watch over the peace," Nimitz declared, "those who fell upon the lonely islands half across the world would have been betrayed." They died to give us "the privilege of living in friendship and decency with other enlightened nations for the present and foreseeable future." Nimitz's passionate appeal perhaps fell on many closed ears. People were tired of war and the talk of war. In the excitement of victory only praise was received — admonishment seldom. This was the day to welcome a hero—not to hold up past failures. They were in no mood for that and seemed to give little heed to the somber warning for the future.

Nimitz left the Capitol and sat high on the seat of the automobile that would carry him by the throngs of his countrymen awaiting to show him their appreciation. The long procession proceeded along Pennsylvania and Constitution Avenues to the Washington Monument. More than half a million citizens, released from their jobs for the occasion, lined the streets to cheer him. Everywhere posters of Nimitz were to be seen — on shop windows, telephone poles, and billboards. A thousand navy fighter planes and bombers flew over the parade, some with red, white, and blue streamers, others in formation spelling NIMITZ.

In the processional were tractors pulling captured Japanese planes, scores of midshipmen, marines, navy nurses, Spars, Waves, and veterans from every naval operation in the South Pacific. When Nimitz reached the Washington Monument he made his second speech of the day. Here he hit hard upon another of his great concerns he wanted the American people to hear. He said, "Perhaps it is not too much to predict that history will refer to this present period, not as the ending of a great conflict, but as the beginning of a new atomic age." He expressed hope that the technologists and scientists were correct in saying that at some "unpredictable" time in the future, atomic power would be "tamed and harnessed" for "industrial and humanitarian uses."

"Our frontiers now," he added, "are the entire world. Before an aggressor can attack us effectively, the attack must come across the sea, either on the surface, underneath the surface, or above the surface. America today realizes that sea power is no longer confined to ships and men, but also includes planes and bases." Nimitz was to emphasize over and over the need for sea power in the future, by explaining its tremendous impact in the conclusion of the war.

The Nimitz party then left the Washington Monument and proceeded to the White House rose garden where President Truman awarded him a gold star in lieu of a third Distinguished Service Medal.

Here Nimitz made his most impassioned statement. He said he accepted the medal on behalf of the more than 2,000,000 men who served under him in the Pacific. It was in tribute to them who through their sacrifice and dedication to duty made the victory possible. So to the sailors, soldiers, marines, and coast guardsmen to whom he saluted in that moment he said to the president, "I accept this honor as your 'well done' to a job that they have done."

It was a touching moment. The huge crowd showed their pleasure with rounds of applause, cheering, and tears.

Later that evening Nimitz and his family with a host of friends, most heroes who fought in defense of their country, attended a gala dinner in his honor.

Nimitz accepted their tribute with humor and humility, prepared as always with the right word at the right moment.

The next day he made a personal call on Secretary of the Navy Forrestal to discuss with him his personal future. As he walked up the steps to the Navy Department he remembered a question his son had asked him years earlier in a conversation they had. Chet asked his father what he really wanted to do in the navy, and the older Nimitz answered, "I want to be Chief of Naval Operations." For Nimitz, holding that office, was like being president of the United States; it was the highest and most prestigious office in the navy. It was his secret goal. He had not mentioned it to anyone else, never feeling it was the wise or appropriate thing to do. It was in truth, however, always in the back of his mind. Every assignment he received he felt helped to prepare him for the job. Now he was ready to assume it.

There were some political obstacles, however. Nimitz and Forrestal had not always seen eye to eye. Nor had Nimitz complied with all of Forrestal's requests of him through the years. A strained relationship had built up between them even while Nimitz was Chief of the Bureau of Navigation. In this position he had openly opposed Forrestal's blatant efforts to push his Wall Street friends into high ranking positions in the navy's administrative posts. A heated feud had arisen when Nimitz purposefully blocked a commission for a civilian friend of Forrestal's who had a prison record. Nimitz declared it was against navy regulations, while Forrestal insisted it was Nimitz's hard-headedness. Later, after the war started and the need for more aviators in important command posts became critical, Forrestal regarded Nimitz as slow and reluctant to make such appointments. Nimitz argued this was not the case. It was simply that he refused to appoint people any faster than they were prepared to assume positions of responsibility. Nimitz and King had made overtures to placate the secretary by recommending the appointment of Admiral Towers as Deputy CinCPac-CinCPOA, Towers being a longtime friend of Forrestal. To add to the bad relations, Nimitz had heard the rumor that Forrestal had tried to secure Admiral King's appointment as commander of the Pacific fleet. This could be construed in either of two ways. One was Forrestal's attempt to get King out of the way in Washington. The other was blocking the appointment of Nimitz. Either one was not looked upon with favor by Nimitz. He viewed the entire matter as political expedience and a personal affront.

All of this left Nimitz in a quandary with the situation now before him. He knew King was soon to retire and the job would be open, but to make his desires known to a man who could easily block his appointment was difficult indeed.

It was a lifelong characteristic of Nimitz to make the direct approach whenever possible. He simply told Forrestal that he would like to succeed Admiral King as Chief of Naval Operations.

Forrestal did not bandy words. He explained he had battled with Admiral King in that position and did not intend to bring in anyone else who would be equally difficult and adamant about their convictions. He told Nimitz he felt it was definitely a mistake to place his name forward as Chief of Naval Operations, suggesting in a weak way that it might diminish the prestige he was now enjoying as the successful commander and hero of the Pacific war. He offered as alternatives either the chairmanship of the general board or simply to remain as commander-in-chief of the Pacific fleet.

Nimitz did not accept the alternatives nor the reason Forrestal proposed. Nimitz stood firm and asked that he be considered for the job. He left Forrestal's office with nothing settled. On Tuesday morning, October 9, Nimitz and his celebrated party moved on to New York and another ticker-tape parade with another host of admirers. The New Yorkers had made up for the lack of a shipboard grandstand and established the honored admiral aboard a replica of a ship's bow at the City Hall Plaza. Mayor Fiorello LaGuardia welcomed Nimitz to New York and presented him with the city's gold medal of honor and a certificate of honorary citizenship.

To a crowd of over 350,000 Nimitz talked about teamwork. "Basically," he said, "the victory was a product of teamwork. We had teamwork among the ground, air, sea, and undersea elements. We had teamwork on the homefront. We adapted ourselves to war; we made radarmen out of boys who had tinkered with radios; we made gunner's mates and coxswains out of youngsters who had never seen the ocean. Some of our best sailors had no more previous experience at sea beyond a ride on the Staten Island ferry. But they performed exceptionally well."

In typical fashion he added his own brand of humor to the occasion. He said, "The ability to learn new jobs was not confined to those in the service. We may joke about the beauty operators who became welders or the accountant who became a riveter, but their adaptability was no joke to the Japanese. It was one cause of Japan's defeat."

Ending his remarks on a serious note, he observed, "We must make certain now and for the future that the peace is secure. We must remain strong. Never again should we risk the threat which weakness invites. We owe this to the men who have fought and to the youngsters who are growing up today."

The crowd roared its approval and a groundswell of thunderous applause was the response of an appreciative audience. A buffet was hosted by Mayor LaGuardia at the Waldorf-Astoria Hotel. More than 2,000 guests gathered to honor and toast the admiral.

In response Nimitz took the opportunity in his opening remarks to tell the crowd about the current song going around about the imaginary sailor named Patty McCoy. The verses were about a cocky sailor's letter to his mother and were written by Captain William Gordon Beecher, Jr., better known as "Slim." The words have been identified primarily as a literary work gleaned from censoring a letter. In introducing the poem, the admiral apologized with a grin for violating the sanctity of postal correspondence. Then he shared with them these words of the song:

Patty McCoy
An American boy
Left his home in the Golden State.
He set off to sea
In a shiny D.D.
And wound up in Task Force Three-eight.

He cruised for a while
With a satisfied smile
Then he took his pencil in hand
And here's what he wrote
In a well-censored note
To his family in state-side land.
Me — and Halsey and Nimitz
Have sure got the Japs on the run,
We're driving 'em wacky
In old Nagasaki
We're settin' the damn Risin' sun.
Kyushu and Kure and Kobe
Are wonderful ruins to see
We got em' like gophers a seeking a hole
The treatment we give 'em is good for the soul.
And everything out here is under control
By Nimitz and Halsey and — me.
Me — and Halsey and Nimitz
Are having a wonderful time
What we ain't uprootin'
By bombin' and shootin'
Would fit on the face of a dime.
They say we're a savin' a nation
And that may be true as can be
They're gettin' a pushin' all over the place
We give 'em the Arsenic — minus the Lace
They're takin' a kickin' — and not in the face
From Nimitz and Halsey — and me.
Me — and Halsey and Nimitz
Are anchored in Tokyo Bay
The place is just drippin'
American shippin'
They stretch for a hell of a way
We hear that the fighting is finished
And that is the way it should be
Remember Pearl Harbor — they started it there

NIMITZ RECEIVES his high school diploma from his old math teacher, John Toland, October, 1945.

We're warning them never to start it again
For we have a country with millions of men
Like Nimitz and Halsey — and me.

The next day Admiral Nimitz returned to Washington. Dissatisfied with the frame of mind and state of affairs he had left Secretary Forrestal in, he returned to his office and found him in somewhat of a changed mood. Apparently many of Nimitz's friends and cohorts had been running some interference for him. Forrestal was feeling the pressure and possibly the wisdom of appointing Nimitz to the prestigious job as Chief of Naval Operations. He did, however, make one more feeble attempt at discouraging Nimitz. He asked him if he really wanted to be tied down to the routine the job would demand. Nimitz was irritated by the nuance in the question that intimated he might not understand what the job entailed as well as enduring another clumsy attempt to dissuade him. His answer to Forrestal was typically Nimitz — courteous, but firm and clear. He replied that he was aware of how exacting the job was, but was confident that he could do the job and do it in an exemplary fashion.

Forrestal relented, but with certain conditions. He said he would recommend Nimitz to the president with these stipulations: First, that his staff would be mutually agreeable to the two of them. Second, that his term would be limited to two years. Three, that he subscribe in general principle to the conception of the Navy Department organization as expressed in the new chart.

Forrestal was making certain Nimitz could not usurp his control nor by-pass him and deal directly with the president. These qualifications presented no real problems to Nimitz. Two years as CNO would be enough for him. And as for the other stipulations, he felt he had always abided by protocol and felt a twinge of insult that Forrestal would include such insinuations in stating his requirements for recommendation to the post.

Again Nimitz left Forrestal's office with mixed emotions. It was evident that they were not in harmony and had little understanding of one another. He felt uneasy about the appointment and the man who had recommended it. He was preparing to leave for a friendlier place. He was on his way to Texas.

For all the fanfare and display of Washington and New York, Texas was preparing its own roundup. Felix McKnight of the Dallas *Morning News* said, the comparison wasn't even close, "Somehow those good folks along Broadway and at the Washington Monument just don't have that Texas touch." Chester Nimitz, who knew a good longhorn steer when he saw one, got his first "yip-yip-yippee" in Dallas, and he loved it. On the corner of Akard and Main there was more bedlam than at any one spot on Broadway. But McKnight lamented, "It wasn't their fault up East — they just never had to holler at a bawling calf or an uppity bronc. It's just the difference between a cheer and a cowboy yell."

For the man who conquered as admiral of the Pacific — the man who admitted that until he went to the Naval Academy his sea experience had been limited to the Guadalupe River — the day couldn't have been more perfect.

Indeed, the snowy-haired Nimitz accepted unconditionally the keys of the city of Dallas, while thousands of fellow citizens watched with awe and respect.

Even so it seemed that nowhere had the public really captured the true importance of what had been accomplished. Jack B. Kruger wrote that "it was the soft-voiced man with the twinkling blue eyes who threw American naval might against the Japanese and brought them to their knees. It took unblemished toughness to do that."

Everyone was willing to declare Nimitz an immortal in Texas history, along with men of the Alamo and San Jacinto, and indeed reserved a spot at the Hall of State at the State Fair grounds where such notables as Fannin, Houston, and Lamar were honored.

BUST OF ADMIRAL Chester W. Nimitz by Felix de Weldon, now on display at the Hall of State, Dallas, Texas.
— *Courtesy Admiral Nimitz State Historical Park*

A silver tea service was presented to Nimitz by the Dallas city fathers and in return the Texas admiral presented the city the five-star insignia he wore aboard the battleship *Missouri* when he signed the documents of peace with Japan.

In his speech at the Hall of State, Nimitz talked first out of his respect and appreciation for those Texans who served so valiantly in the Pacific and for those who held the faith at home. He insisted that though he was the one being honored all the brave men and women regardless of service affiliation should receive the tribute. It was a great team, but in the Pacific it was obvious that the job could never have been done without sea power. He added that he hoped that in the future our country will always be in a position to exercise sea power when it is needed, where it is needed, and in strength sufficient to guarantee the nation's safety.

Admiral Nimitz in a confidential tone then told the Texans gathered the secret reasons why he felt the Japanese met defeat. First, he said, it was the joint staff that provided a unified command for the army, navy, and marines. Secondly, it was the method of using one fleet as two battle groups. While the commanding officers of one group, far from the rigors of battle, made their plans for new strikes, the other group was battling the enemy. After a task force accomplished its mission the roles were reversed. The third reason, he went on, was our ability to supply our forces at sea with what he called floating bases. These were the supply ships, some of which were constructed to provide dry dock facilities for damaged ships of the fleet. Here ships could be repaired without the long return to Pearl Harbor. This one operation was to keep the fleet at the scene of action and reduce the time span which would otherwise have been required to transverse the wide expanse of the Pacific Ocean. Without seapower, Nimitz forcefully proclaimed, we could have never advanced in the war of the Pacific as we did.

The ovation Nimitz received was louder than the "Eyes of Texas" that played in the background, and as the admiral walked out into the streets to continue to the Baker Hotel for lunch, the more than 300,000 people in one way or another tried to say "hi" or touch his sleeve. McKnight noted the expressions on many faces along the way: "I saw joy; I saw pride; I saw respect; I saw tears. I did not see a pair of eyes that were not riveted to the strong features of the man who took the hardest job any individual had in this war and turned it into an ephochal triumph."

The day, however, was not over for the Nimitz party. After lunch he was whisked away to catch a plane to Austin where again there were speeches, gifts, and banquets to honor him. Governor Coke Stevenson and Congressman Lyndon B. Johnson joined the admiral as the group paraded after dark along the route of 10,000 Christmas lights illumined for the occasion. It was late into the night, after much display of admiration, before Admiral and Mrs. Nimitz went to bed for the first time in many years, in their home state of Texas. It was indeed a night and a day to remember.

The next day, Saturday, October 13, the Nimitz party made their way by car to Fredericksburg, Nimitz's birthplace, and to Kerrville, his boyhood home. Again the governor and congressman joined them, together with Rear Admiral Sherman, and Rear Admiral Harold B. Miller, the Navy Department's Public Relations Officer.

There was a mixture of pride and humility as he returned in fulfillment of his grandfather's dream and his own boyhood promise when he left for Annapolis in 1901 to return someday as an admiral. However, his return as a world-celebrated hero was more than he had pledged. Among the bands, drum corps, and marching units were soldiers, sailors, and veterans along with members of the German community who in the jubilation of the moment were caught up in an enthusiasm that their stoic heritage normally did not make allowances for. It was evident their feelings were deep and strong. Many were saying, "Ol' Cap'n Nimitz's boy has come back to the hills of home." The older folks said he was the "spittin' " image of his grandfather and with tremendous pride for a native son they turned out to do him honor.

The greeting in Kerrville was more than just a hero's welcome. The outpouring of love and affection could only be matched by the gratitude and admiration that comes from kinsmen — the sturdy German stock from which he was born. It was a demonstration for one of their own, a person who had grown in stature to a position that ranked him among the true notables of the world. Yet it was evident to all that he had retained the common touch and genuine concern for his family and friends. Honors were piled one upon another in words of praise, flowers, and gifts, but the real welcome came in the handshakes, their backslaps, the hugs and kisses of old friends, schoolmates, teachers, and relatives. The "Hill Country" was alive with exaltation.

The famed admiral was touched deeply, his voice always low, often choked from time to time as he was overcome by the emotion and nostalgia created by those moments. He said simply, "It's good to be home again."

FAMILY REUNION photograph taken at home of Otto Nimitz in Kerrville.

He told them of his war experiences and how happy he was, as any sailor would be, to be back again with his own kind.

Almost before he could finish what he had to say . . . the surprise came. His favorite teacher, Mrs. Susan Moore, came forward together with Superintendent of Schools H. A. Moore, and Chester W. Nimitz was awarded his high school diploma, forty-two years late by John G. Toland, his old math teacher. It was said that it was the first time a person had received a Phi Beta Kappa key before they had received a high school diploma. The University of Texas had given Nimitz the key the night before at the victory celebration in Austin.

In his remarks to hometown friends he reiterated how good it was to be among them and to be back in the Hill Country he had always remembered as home. He confessed that he only had one real concern while signing the armistice document in Tokyo Bay and that was: whether Texas would agree to it, wondering whether they would rather continue fighting or sign a separate peace.

After lunch the admiral and his party retraced their steps back to Fredericksburg and the old Nimitz Hotel. There they were participants in a celebration that rivaled the one in Kerrville. Being his birthplace, the Fredericksburg greeting was tumultuous, with more parades, more noise, more marching units, more everything . . . even more emotional and more reminiscent of bygone days. Stories were told again and again about the young admiral-to-be as they recalled his boyhood. His sister, Dora Reagan, recalled the many funny things that happened in the old hotel, especially Grandfather Nimitz's room. She said, "I saw my first Roman candle there one Christmas. Chester shot it off. If he puts out the fires in the Pacific as quick as we put out the fire from that candle everything would be all right."

One friend recalled him being a daring lad who loved pranks, and spoke of the time he slipped behind the bass viol player at the old hotel ballroom and held the music so it couldn't be turned. The old man sawed away while he tugged at the music all to no avail. Another remembered how Chester could take any bump on the head, however hard, but let him cut his finger even slightly and he howled to no end.

Another friend remembering Kerrville days said that one time a couple of Schreiner Institute boys put Chester up to placing a mirror in the chicken yard where fine gamecocks were kept. One of the birds almost knocked his brains out trying to get to the bird in the mirror.

Stories, stories, and more stories of the famed admiral circulated, but none so poignant or humorous as his own. Nimitz's roots were deep and firm in the solid stone of the Hill Country. Years and distance had not wrenched the old-time German customs so deeply embedded in the people of the "Hill Country." Nimitz had kept the record personally of the family. His sister Dora remarked to friends that "he kept a book for both sides of the family and he wanted to know when any of them married or had babies. "Why, one time when he was here," she said, "we had a reception and he met many of them for the first time. No matter, he called them all by name and he had all the new ones stand in a group so he could meet them and would be able to remember their names the next time he came to Fredericksburg."

As Fleet Admiral Nimitz was about to take his leave of family and friends and the scenes of his boyhood, he was asked a question publicly that many were asking privately: "Will you be appointed as the next Chief of Naval Operations?"

Nimitz answered only as he could: "That is not for me to say, nor for me to answer. It is not in my power to decide."

Indeed it wasn't and the outcome was causing him some anxiety, but he would not allow anything to diminish this warm and glorious moment in his life.

Yes, Old Captain Nimitz's boy Chester had come back to the limestone bluff of Tivy Mountain and the valleys of the Pedernales and the Guadalupe rivers, to the streams and to the sturdy folks who were a vital part of the proud people of Texas.

FLEET ADMIRAL CHESTER NIMITZ poses with Texans who held the Congressional Medal of Honor at the Texas State Fair in Dallas in 1946.
— *Official U.S. Navy photo.*
Courtesy Admiral Nimitz State Historical Park

FLEET ADMIRAL NIMITZ makes a speech on board the USS *Missouri* while at the navy yard in Boston on September 2, 1946, after the signing of the surrender by the Japanese Royal Navy in Tokyo Bay.
— *Official U.S. Navy photo.*
Courtesy Admiral Nimitz State Historical Park

16

Permission to Go Ashore

Fleet Admiral Chester Nimitz was back at Pearl Harbor within five days after he left Fredericksburg. There was still much to do making final reports, securing the fleet and arranging for the massive return of more than two million service men — *Operation Magic Carpet* it was called. As Nimitz had explained to anxious loved ones across the country, it takes a lot more time to transfer men back from the Pacific than it does from the Atlantic. He again pleaded for patience.

In a matter of days, Nimitz, King, and Forrestal released statements calling for maintenance of the "greatest naval forces the world has ever known." More ships had been built and sailed in World War II than had ever sailed before. To scrap them would be against all that Nimitz held in trust with the American people. This attitude, however, was not the same as Washington's. He had learned that President Truman had not used the battleship *Missouri* after all in the trip to New York, and instead had insisted upon a destroyer. He made his speech from a hastily erected platform in New York's Central Park. Even though it was Navy Day, Truman's speech had elements of discontent with the navy subtly sprinkled throughout. The president mentioned mostly the victory in Europe and continually praised Army General George C. Marshall. He ended his speech with the hope that he could persuade the navy to begin cooperating with the army.

The entire attitude of the speech was pro-army and the navy came off looking like a stepchild. Nimitz received the message and took the hint. The navy was definitely not priority with Truman — all the more reason Nimitz thought to push for the CNO assignment.

Another issue clouded the decision, however. During the last two years Admiral Nimitz had achieved somewhat of a model of unification among the services and he had more than a year earlier recommended the idea on a national basis. He favored a single Secretary of the Armed Forces with the complete elimination of civilian secretaries of the army, navy, and air force. He was for one commander of the armed forces over all the services with full authority and responsibility. Nimitz had strongly spoken out again and again that the war in the Pacific was won by teamwork.

Now these ideas could be working against his own situation. This was unfortunate since Nimitz in the meantime had changed his mind. Over a year before when it appeared that the unification concept might be put into effect, MacArthur loomed at that time as one who might assume the dominant strategic role, allowing the army to shape organization and strategy, to the detriment of the other branches of the armed forces.

Nor had MacArthur ever understood Nimitz's

projection of advancing across the central part of the Pacific, and Nimitz knew why. It could only be done by ship and by air. The walking army could not be included. Nimitz, therefore, concluded that one single man should not have such power and perhaps a person, not directly involved with either branch of service, would be better suited and more fairly fulfill the task of direct command. Now that much publicity was going to MacArthur as the commander designated for the invasion of Japan, as conductor of the surrender ceremony, and as commander-in-chief of the occupation forces, Nimitz knew he must, with all diligence, protect the integrity and position of the navy. He was honor bound to do all he could to assure the fact that he, himself would become the new Chief of Naval Operations. He felt anything less might be disastrous for the future status of the navy.

Pearl Harbor was not exactly the place to pull strings. Much was going on in Washington on a moment-by-moment basis. Other appointments were pending and as much as he hated to admit it Nimitz did not trust Forrestal, or for that matter President Truman. Had Knox and President Roosevelt still been in office this appointment would be assured. As it was, rumors were flying that Forrestal had changed his mind and Nimitz was out.

By sheer luck an old friend arrived in Honolulu by the name of William Waldo Drake. Early in the war, Drake had been Nimitz's public relations officer. He was now working for Edwin Pauley, President Truman's representative on the Allied Reparations Commission. Pauley had been the man who put Harry Truman in the White House, and Nimitz was sure there were due bills.

Nimitz asked Drake to bring Pauley out to Pearl Harbor. This he did, since he was en route to

ADMIRAL LOUIS E. DENFELD reads his acceptance speech as he becomes Chief of Naval Operations when Fleet Admiral Nimitz resigned December 15, 1947.
— *Official U.S. Navy photo.*
Courtesy Admiral Nimitz State Historical Park

Japan anyway, but Pauley was skeptical of the true intent of the admiral and asked that they have a private conversation.

Nimitz and Pauley left the headquarters and drove down to the beach where they could be alone to talk. After a lengthy conversation, the persuasive admiral convinced his new friend of the importance of his being appointed the next Chief of Naval Operations. Immediately, Pauley went back to the headquarters and put in a direct call to the White House, something few men could do, and made his suggestion to President Truman. Truman's answer was less than flattering. He told Pauley, "Well, I'd like to help him, but Forrestal insists he's just a stubborn Dutchman and neither relates to the job nor does Forrestal want him to have it."

As Nimitz had suspected, it was Forrestal who was holding up the appointment, and Truman was going along with it. Nimitz's future was in jeopardy.

In a week's time Nimitz was on his way back to Washington to do three things: rally the naval leaders behind him, appear before the Senate committee, and explain his new position. He had no intention of letting the navy get the run-around. Now more than at any other time the navy needed its strongest spokesman.

Being one who was not reluctant to apologize for changing his mind he addressed the committee forthrightly. "For my part I am now convinced that a single department will not work as efficiently as two separate departments have proved they can work in producing the kinds of forces required for modern war. I am also convinced that the merging of the War and Navy Departments into a single department cannot help, and may hinder, the adequate provision and efficient use of our sea power."

Nimitz spoke with conviction with a heavy stress on sea power, reiterating what he had been saying all across the country, that sea power won the war in the Pacific.

As he made his plea for continued naval armament, he also took the opportunity to make a personal plea. He made a call on the president. Mr. Truman had invited him in when he knew Nimitz was returning to Washington and Nimitz did not hesitate to comply. The meeting was so private no records have been found of the conversation. Only conclusions can be drawn.

FLEET ADMIRAL NIMITZ rides in the inaugural parade of President Harry S Truman and Vice President Alben W. Barkley in Washington, D.C.
— *Official U.S. Navy photo.*
Courtesy Admiral Nimitz State Historical Park

The next day, November 20, President Truman held a press conference and announced the top military appointments for peacetime: General Eisenhower would succeed General Marshall as army chief of staff; Admiral Nimitz would succeed Admiral King as chief of naval operations.

Nimitz's appointment was effective immediately, leaving him with almost no time to move his family to Washington or take adequate leave of his responsibilities at Pearl Harbor. Forrestal was so displeased with the appointment and with Admiral King for forcing his hand with the president that he called for the immediate transfer of authority. Forrestal was eager to see King retire and leave the department. Conversely, he was not so eager to have

Nimitz take his place. The man had troubles. Possessed with strange and foreboding suspicions, he was constantly at odds with the men with whom he worked.

The days of association with Nimitz would be no different.

As the new CNO, Nimitz ran his office much as he had run his fleet, with full authority and discipline. Nimitz included Forrestal in all major conferences, meetings, and decisions, and on the surface the two men appeared to work as a team. Nimitz worked hard at getting along with all his co-workers. The fact that Forrestal was a civilian and an appointee of the president presented its own problems; yet Nimitz took the time and the effort to work with and through the troubled mind and ways of the secretary. Actually, Nimitz never worked as hard.

Bringing the boys home and demobilizing the armed forces was a seven-day-a-week job. The public sentiment to get the men back home quickly put undue time limitations on decommissioning ships and peacetime reorganization. What was true in the Navy Department was true throughout the country. Congress was cutting back on defense spending and appropriations right and left. Staffs were being cut and Washington was fast becoming evacuated.

In addition to his heavy office duties, Nimitz was asked to speak on many occasions. This he was glad to do. He was acting as sort of a public relations man for both the navy and the country. Every major organization that met for the next two years invited Nimitz to speak. Some of the speeches he wrote himself; others he had written for him. This attention to public demand perhaps was one of the most important things Nimitz did while CNO. He spread the word, told the story, and educated the people of America about the war, its operations, and the need for peace. The nation was stunned over the impact of the atom bomb. They questioned its use as a weapon, its humanitarian aspects, and the deployment of it as a means of progress toward peace. Many myths and misconceptions were rampant as to the exact plans for the bomb either for war or peace.

Socially, Nimitz and his wife acquired many new friends. Totally ignoring Forrestal's restrictions that the CNO should not contact the president and vice versa, Mr. Truman frequently called Nimitz to the White House for business and pleasure.

In return the Admiral and Mrs. Nimitz invited the Trumans to their house for dinner and often a game of horseshoes.

One time when the president came, complete with a complement of Secret Service men, Chester took him upstairs and lent him a pair of old khaki pants to wear for the horseshoe game. The two couples generally teamed up with each other's spouse and more times than not Bess Truman and Chester Nimitz won.

The fame of Nimitz's horseshoe playing spread across the country and even became known internationally. One day the world's champion horseshoe pitcher appeared at the admiral's office in the Navy Department. The young man asked, after he had identified himself, if he might have an autographed picture of the admiral.

An aide, knowing the nature of his boss, responded cordially, "I'm sure he is going to want to meet you."

And he did, plus the president of the United States. Chester Nimitz was so impressed with the champion that he called directly to the White House and said, "Harry, I've got the champion horseshoe pitcher of the world in my office. We're coming over to the White House and show you how he can pitch."

PRESIDENT TRUMAN and Admiral Nimitz visited frequently when Nimitz returned to Washington after the war.
— *Official U.S. Navy photo.
Courtesy Admiral Nimitz State Historical Park*

In fifteen minutes Nimitz entered the garden behind the White House with the champion in tow. Truman had canceled his engagements and met him there. The Secret Service men stood amazed as well as amused as they watched three men attempting all sorts of trick and fancy horsehoe pitching.

No doubt, because of the close friendship with the Trumans, the Nimitzes were invited to the White House when the prime minister of England was in town. Winston Churchill had been in Florida vacationing and when he arrived in Washington he requested an opportunity to meet Admiral Nimitz.

The dinner went smoothly with light and jovial conversation as the wives were present. Afterwards, while Churchill enjoyed his brandy and cigar, he pulled Nimitz aside and asked a curious question. "What," asked Churchill, "was your lowest point in the war?" Historians and biographers can speculate on the admiral's answer as well as that of Churchill with insight into both characters; but the question, though never answered publicly, sparked an open and lengthy exchange that lasted almost two hours. The two men had found rapport and had spent an evening enjoying themselves in reflective remembrance.

One of the first things Nimitz did after he became CNO was to contact Admiral Spruance, the new CinCPac, and request the naval commanders in the western Pacific to collect Japanese bells found among the scrapped metal on the mainland of Japan. During the war the Japanese had major drives for scrap metal similar to the ones in the United States. And in time the Japanese were so short of metal that it had to be taken from churches, temples, and other sacrificial shrines. Some of them were priceless relics.

Periodically a bell would show up in Washington at the Navy Department and Nimitz would take the time and interest to look it over. One day a particularly interesting bell showed up with Japanese characters all over it. It weighed at least two hundred pounds and was strikingly beautiful.

When Nimitz saw it he knew it was special. He said he could not keep the bell; it had to go back to Fukuoka where it belonged. This was one of the first gestures of peace started by Admiral Nimitz.

The bell did go back, to the congregation of the First Christian Church in Fukuoka. The people were so impressed and grateful they sent a special acknowledgment through their minister to Admiral Nimitz. The admiral was convinced that in peace as in war small details could make the difference between success and failure.

One of the most unpleasant assignments of a CNO was to be the officer presiding over a court-martial. This was a task Nimitz never enjoyed yet he met them with as much fairness and human understanding as possible. When the admiral took over as CNO, the court-martial of Captain Charles McVay of the cruiser *Indianapolis* was in progress. McVay was accused of losing his ship to the enemy and Nimitz had vehementy spoken out against the need for such a trial in the first place, feeling it was totally unnecessary. Forrestal, however, was adamant and the trial took place.

McVay was acquitted of the charge for failing to issue orders to abandon ship in time, but was found guilty of failing to evade the enemy. After the trial was over Nimitz called a press conference.

Not hedging on the truth, Nimitz said openly. "We have no desire or intention to deny any of our mistakes ... but we advocate clemency and the Secretary of the Navy has remitted the sentence of Captain McVay in its entirety, releasing him from arrest and restoring him to duty."

Newsmen, being who they are, probed further. One asked, concerned about the captain's future in the navy, "Has there ever been a court-martialed officer in the history of the U.S. Navy who was later promoted to flag rank?"

Nimitz could not keep a straight face. "Here's one," he said and broke up the entire news conference. With humor and good fun the admiral told his true story of the incident thirty-eight years back when he had been court-martialed for grounding the *Decatur*.

The two years as Chief of Naval Operations passed quickly. For Nimitz it was tiring. He spent his days at the office when he was not traveling or making speeches. At the last of his tenure he began to write for national publications concerning the war and his desire for peace. He had become intensely involved with the testing and the effect of atomic weapons on warships and began to make a study of the controversy that surrounded the use of atomic power. In March, 1946, the spring before Nimitz left his post, the Naval Research Laboratory distributed a report recommending the construction of a nuclear-powered submarine. In less than six months the project was scuttled. Nimitz approved instead the design of "nuclear-power" plans for research and development. This project was given top priority.

While in Washington the Nimitz household grew. Both Chet, Jr. and Kate were busy becoming parents, making Catherine and Chester happy grandparents. It was a role that suited Chester. He enjoyed walking the children in the park and showing them off to friends and interested newsmen. Their youngest daughter, Mary, was in school in California and the family was learning once more to be a family unit. Chester Nimitz was a happy, but a disturbed man.

In spite of all his speeches to both the public and the private sector as well as before congressional committees and in official hearings, the navy was being continually cut back. Beautiful and serviceable ships were being scrapped and retired. The stately, powerful fleet was being sent into mothballs and all his projections for a strong navy continually guarding the shores of the country were slowly but surely fading away. On November 12, 1947, one month before his tour as Chief of Naval Operations was to end, the doggedly persistent admiral made his final plea. He testified before the president's Air Policy Committee, stating that the navy should have all 5,793 planes at its constant disposal and warned that the naval protection strength was "dangerously low."

The next day without warning or explanation President Truman announced the appointment of Admiral Louis E. Denfeld as the new Chief of Naval Operations.

Chester Nimitz was disappointed, but relieved. All his efforts on behalf of the navy seemed to have failed, yet for the first time he felt a great burden had been lifted from his shoulders. He had carried the responsibility of all naval operations and personnel personally. He was visibly and understandably tired. He had fulfilled almost every role any naval officer could fill. He had commanded ships, taught officers, directed war strategy, and acted as a diplomat, statesman, and protocol officer. He had trod the decks of ships both large and small, sailed on every sea, and fought in two great world wars. He had dealt with the common sailor and supreme commanders of the world. He had done a good job. Now he was ready to rest.

For the first time Admiral Nimitz could be the family man he had wanted to be. They could buy a home, entertain friends, be a part of a community, enjoy the cultural amenities, and share some life together.

So back to California they went ... Catherine and Chester Nimitz, Nancy and Freckles, the aging cocker spaniel, and the old car Chrissy ... to settle down.

But it was not to be for long.

ADMIRAL CHESTER NIMITZ (top) and his party attend the Metropolitan Opera opening November 11, 1946, in New York. With Admiral and Mrs. Nimitz are the Thomas J. Watsons.
— *Courtesy Admiral Nimitz State Historical Park*

ADMIRAL NIMITZ shown with the powerful binoculars in the garden of his home at 728 Santa Barbara Road, Berkeley, California, during the mid-1950s.
— *Courtesy Admiral Nimitz State Historical Park*

17

Old Admirals Never Retire

At sixty-two Chester Nimitz and his wife of thirty-four years landed again in California, this time to set up housekeeping on a permanent basis. They had never owned a home and were genuinely looking forward to it. Since five-star admirals and generals never retire, Nimitz was happy to settle for trading in his dress blues for a pair of khaki shorts and sneakers. He wanted to go back into gardening, enjoying his grandchildren, and spending some time in civic affairs.

In San Francisco, the admiral was furnished an office in the 12th Naval District headquarters in the Federal Building. This gave him a base of operation but without formal duties. There he received his mail, answered his calls, and conducted necessary business. He was still very active as a speaker and was pleased to accommodate schools and universities on short notice. He talked mostly of peace. It was a growing theme for him and he had visions of what he considered to be a way to sure and lasting peace. For the most part, it was an extension of his own philosophy of life, as well an appreciation of his fellowman and respect for their contributions.

For the first several months the Nimitzes lived in the San Francisco Bay area in a hotel, but soon moved across the bay to the Claremont Hotel in Berkeley. Their real concern at this particular time was to find a house that would suit their needs.

Finally, in May of the next year the right house appeared, complete with all the requirements desired by Nimitz himself. It must have three bathrooms, he decreed, and overlook the sea. They found such a place and instantly loved it. In Berkeley, nestled back on Santa Barbara Road along with other attractive homes, this house had a living room, dining room, and breakfast room all facing westward with the blue waters of San Francisco Bay, framing perfectly the Golden Gate Bridge.

Mrs. Nimitz said the admiral instantly became a "mad gardener," planting everything he could think of and building compost heaps to supply the soil with nourishment. In time the yard and garden became a galaxy of color.

Soon, like many other retired people settling in the bay area, Chester and Catherine became a vital part of the community. They attended concerts, entertained friends, and their children gradually moved closer to them. They had everything to make them happy; good health, children nearby, and good friends to visit. No one would have said the admiral did not deserve the rest and release from responsibility. In the midst of such gracious living Chester Nimitz was invited back to Washington for President Truman's first inauguration.

He was honored and quickly accepted.

The Secretary of Navy, John L. Sullivan, sent his personal plane to pick up Nimitz and return him to Washington. Admiral Halsey and General Archer

Vandegrift were also invited. The three leaders from the Pacific Theater sat together on the platform to observe Harry Truman take the oath of office as president of the United States. This time Mr. Truman had been elected by the people in an overwhelming and surprising victory. Nimitz stayed for the parade and rode in one of the official cars. He later attended the reception honoring Truman and then boarded the plane back to California.

The trip proved to be far more significant than Nimitz had expected. He thought he was simply returning to Washington to be with a good friend at his brightest hour. He was not prepared for what was to come.

In less than two months a dispatch would come from Admiral Denfeld, the CNO, asking if he was interested in being the Supervisor of Elections in Kashmir for the United Nations, to determine whether that state should join Pakistan or India.

Of course Nimitz was interested. He was a man of peace as well as an experienced negotiator. This was how he could further his own personal efforts toward peace and advance that cause in other parts of the world. Besides, what an adventure in another part of the world. His response to action came about as quickly as his former response to leisure. He was ready to go. Always a man dedicated to his country, he reacted to a call of duty without hesitation. He was ready.

When he arrived in Washington Nimitz was quickly briefed on the Kashmir situation. In 1947 Pakistan had separated itself from India leaving the state of Kashmir without a government. The Maharaja of Kashmir favored union with India but this did not please the Moslems of Pakistan who wanted the territory of Kashmir. In expression of their displeasure they invaded Kashmir and threatened its capital, Srinagar, with destruction. In response, the Maharaja quickly aligned his state with India and appealed for their military aid. India flew troops to Kashmir on a continuing basis for the next eighteen months to combat periodic wars that flared up almost daily. Finally, India appealed the case to the United Nations Security Council. The Security Council issued an immediate cease-fire decree and mandated that the future of Kashmir would be determined by plebiscite with the will of the people deciding. Both countries, India and Pakistan, agreed to negotiate a truce on that basis and agreed to withdraw their troops from Kashmir in order to make provisions for the plebiscite. This was the election Admiral Nimitz was to administer.

Within a matter of days Nimitz had conferred with the State Department, Pakistani and Indian diplomats, and government officials from many other countries. He picked his staff from representatives of the United Nations: Canada, France, China, and Great Britain, and learned from plebiscite experts the rules of international elections. He was preparing to leave for India the latter part of April, but was advised by the State Department to wait until the truce agreements had been completed and formally signed. These agreements seemed to be plagued by discontented leaders. Both nations continued to find fault and raise objections. Over and over again the time of departure was pushed further and further into the future. In the meantime, Nimitz took advantage of the opportunity to learn more about international negotiations.

By June, the countries still could not get together on a truce agreement and Nimitz began to suspect that the plebiscite would never be allowed to be held. He suggested to the secretary-general that his staff be dissolved and he stay on alone until the situation could be solved one way or another.

In August Nimitz was requested to arbitrate a truce in Kashmir, itself, and to draw up an agreement immediately. When the prime minister of India, Jawaharlal Nehru, heard of this he was enraged. Consequently, all joint meetings scheduled to begin in New Delhi the following week were cancelled. Nimitz admitted it was now a matter for the Security Council.

President Truman wrote to the prime ministers of both nations to again consider accepting Admiral Nimitz's arbitration. Nehru rejected it on the premise that it was "American intervention."

For two months the situation stood unresolved, but Nehru was coming to the United States for a visit and there were hopes for some meeting of minds at that time.

Unfortunately, this did not occur. Nehru was not the congenial guest. He was defensive, difficult, and unbending. All efforts to encourage him to open up conversations about Kashmir and in general to establish some kind of understanding failed. Nimitz met with him three times, without making any progress concerning resolution of the Kashmir situations. Nehru would only consider the issue if the United States would favor India. Any attempt at considering the position of Pakistan was not tolerated by the prime minister.

Nimitz reported the visit a lost cause and the issue of a plebiscite unworkable. In the end the Security Council voted to replace the United Nations Commission for India and Pakistan with a one-man U.N. representative.

His return this time was to be the last by his own choice. While he was in New York the political world of Nimitz drastically changed. Forrestal had committed suicide, the Secretaries of the Navy,

Defense, and State had all been changed. The pending war in Korea had proven Nimitz to be right in his adamant stand for continuous readiness of all services and in a critical moment President Truman called Nimitz at his home in New York and asked if he would consider returning to active duty and take over once more the job of Chief of Naval Operations.

Nimitz politely refused, saying he would only come back if ordered. His reasoning was that he believed a younger man should have the job and recommended his friend, Admiral Forrest Sherman.

When Nimitz reached California he learned that the president had followed his recommendation and Sherman had been appointed.

He resigned his formal position with the United Nations with a feeling he had headed a fruitless mission to Kashmir. It was a mission, as he saw it, that never really left the halls of the United Nations. In statements later made to a news reporter, he concluded: "India and Pakistan together could be a powerful influence in Asia, but India has resisted pressure to resolve the dispute."

This man who had believed and worked for peace returned home with the threat of war again on the horizon. He returned with one small toe in the international door. Secretary-General Trygve Lie persuaded Nimitz to stay on with the United Nations as a roving "good-will ambassador." He consented and over the next two years spoke in nearly every state in the Union concerning the issues and work within the United Nations.

Adjusting to California life was easy and pleasant, but Chester Nimitz maintained a strong and lively feeling for his home state of Texas. In April 1961 he made his final trip to his native "Hill Country."

Vice-President Lyndon Johnson invited Nimitz to be his guest at the LBJ Ranch, along with his guest, German Chancellor Konrad Adenauer. Being of German heritage and a native of Texas, Secretary of State Dean Rusk urged Nimitz to accept. He didn't need to be urged. He was ready almost at any time to have an excuse to return to Texas and especially Fredericksburg.

The visit was a huge success. It wasn't every day a German leader came to the Hill Country. Nearly 7,000 German-Texans greeted their guest. Adenauer surprised them all. Tall, thin, and agile for his eighty-five years he spoke, sang, ate Texas food, and wore a Texas hat. Adenauer spoke to the gathering in German, while Johnson and Nimitz made their remarks in English. They then toured the city, each in a separate limousine. Adenauer was interested in seeing the older homes of the first settlers of Fredericksburg; Nimitz was interested in visiting relatives. However, when the honored guests were ready to leave to helicopter back to the LBJ Ranch, the admiral was not to be found. The Secret Service men who were responsible for Nimitz's safety had taken him to the hospital to visit his two sick aunts, *Tante* Lise and *Tante* Minni. Nimitz apologized but was happy enough to let the distinguished dignitaries go on ahead of him. He would catch up with them after he had seen the people who were a part of his heritage.

Perhaps there was some premonition in the old admiral's thoughts. This trip to Texas proved to be his last one. Never again was he to set foot on the soil he had loved for so many years — the Texas "Hill Country," where his roots were deep and lasting.

The unexpected that had followed Chester Nimitz throughout his life managed to prevail to the last. In 1963, while at his office in San Francisco, Nimitz fell and broke his kneecap. This accident required surgery and a lengthy recuperation. Afterwards he was able to walk, but continued to have severe pain in his right hip and lower back. This continued until surgery was called for again and at that time the diagnosis was osteoarthritis of the spine.

Nimitz's doctor insisted that he was much too old for such long and extensive surgery, especially when there was no guarantee of success. Nevertheless, the admiral wanted it. Without hesitating Catherine concurred. "Go ahead and do it, if he wanted it," she told the physician in charge.

The surgery was successful, but while he was in the hospital he developed pneumonia. Soon he suffered a series of small strokes and showed signs of congestive heart failure. All in all, the admiral was very ill. Chester, Jr., aware of the seriousness of his father's condition, suggested that he be taken home. On December 11, with much insistence from the family, the trip was made. With his indomitable spirit and incredible will to live he celebrated the Christmas holidays that had always meant so much to him. With Catherine, his children, and his grandchildren around him, the spirit of *tannenbaum* and Kris Kringle was experienced for the last time. He enjoyed watching the bowl games on New Year's Day, and then quietly and peacefully on Sunday, February 20, with Catherine by his side, he slipped away.

Three days later, February 24, 1966, Chester Nimitz's eighty-first birthday, he lay in state in the Treasure Island Naval Station Chapel. That afternoon a motorcade of more than one hundred vehicles escorted the Fleet Admiral to his final resting place, the Golden Gate National Cemetery. As the caisson reached the grave, seventy navy jets flew over and a nineteen-gun salute rang through the cool crisp air as a final tribute to one of America's greatest heroes of all time.

EPILOGUE

Chester W. Nimitz in his latter years became as committed to world peace as he had ever been committed to war. Never one to take up arms unnecessarily, he constantly strove for peace; but with the passing of the years he came to see more and more clearly the absolute need for every effort to be made for keeping the peace.

After World War II, Nimitz personally devoted his efforts to making every possible overture for peace with Japan and the Japanese people. As an early devotee of Admiral Heihachiro Togo, he had a warm place in his heart for the Japanese. Even before the final surrender was confirmed by the formal signatures of the Allied forces on the deck of the *Missouri,* Nimitz made a visit to the *Mikasa.* The *Mikasa* was the flagship of Admiral Togo, famed commander of the Japanese fleet in the Russo-Japanese War of 1905, who destroyed the Russian fleet at the battle of Tsushima. When Nimitz visited the ship it had been stripped of its valuable brass and copper fittings due to the Japanese war effort which salvaged everything possible for the manufacture of armaments. The Japanese had kept it as a shrine and a national monument. Without hesitation Nimitz ordered security guards to be stationed at the gangplank to secure the vessel from vandalism.

He later led a movement to restore the vessel to

its original condition as far as possible, and made his own contribution to further this effort.

Nimitz also understood the value placed by the Japanese on their personal swords. In his forty years as a navy officer he had collected a number of beautiful swords, knives, and ceremonial daggers from his travels around the world. Among them were three Japanese swords that were presented to him after the surrender. After an appropriate period of time, Nimitz returned these swords in a gesture of peace and good will. Admiral E.M. Eller, in relating the lesser known contributions to peace by Nimitz, said, "It is not wealth that makes a nation great, but the virtues of its people. In peace as well as in war Admiral Nimitz exemplified the true spirit of service to the state, so profoundly set forth by Pericles: 'I would have you day by day fix your eyes upon the greatness of Athens, until you become filled with the love of her; and when you are impressed by the spectacle of her glory, reflect that this empire has been acquired by men who knew duty and had the courage to do it.'"

In return the Japanese people sent a contingent of men, expert in Japanese gardening, to the United States to build a garden in memory of Admiral Nimitz and Admiral Togo. Using local rock, unique plantings, and elaborate landscape designs, seven Japanese moved to Fredericksburg, Texas, for six months, to build the Garden of Peace at the Nimitz Center. The garden now stands as a symbol of friendship and peace between America and Japan. Because of their admiration for Nimitz the people of Japan subscribed the funds to build the garden behind the Nimitz Steamboat Hotel. The garden features the classic Japanese style with a replica of Admiral Togo's study. Along the tree-lined walk are benches where people can stop and rest, think, and meditate. In spite of the fact that Admiral Nimitz was the architect for the Japanese defeat in the Pacific, his kindnesses that followed, as evidenced by his returning the *samurai* swords, his insistence that the bells be returned to the various churches to whom they belonged, and his leadership in restoring the *Mikasa* battleship, as their national monument, all contributed to respect for Nimitz the man and cemented the dream of peace that the Japanese shared with him.

But peace exacts a price — that Chester Nimitz would be the first to admit. That price is dedication and sacrifice, the same as the price for victory in battle; but how much greater is the significance of fighting for peace. After the bitter and costly war against the Japanese Empire, Nimitz was able to firmly state, "I am not in favor of preventive war. I believe in using diplomatic means as long as there is any chance of success. Peace can be attained, but we will have to show courage and patience and skill."

A short time before his death, Chester Nimitz was being interviewed for a story to be published in a national magazine. His remarks deserve attention from one generation to another.

"Last November 7, I remarked to my Marine Corps driver, 'Today is a very special day for me because it was just sixty-three years ago I entered the Naval Academy.'

"Well, admiral, do you think you will make a career of it?" he quipped.

"Yes, I think I shall," I told him. "I'm still learning every day. I still try to do my best and I refuse to worry about things over which I have no control. If I had a chance to live my life over again I'd still follow Grandfather Nimitz's philosophy — even if it led to another court-martial."

ADMIRAL NIMITZ examines a captured Japanese sword in his home in Berkeley, California.
— *Courtesy Admiral Nimitz State Historical Park*

Epilogue

A RELAXED NIMITZ
— *Courtesy Admiral Nimitz State Historical Park*

284   ADMIRAL OF THE HILLS

U.S. NAVAL ACADEMY at Annapolis, Maryland. At the top is an artist's portrayal of the Academy at the turn of the century when Admiral Nimitz was a midshipman. Below is an aerial view of the Academy as it appeared in 1982.

— *Official U.S. Navy photo, courtesy Captain Roy C. Smith III, USNR (Ret.)*

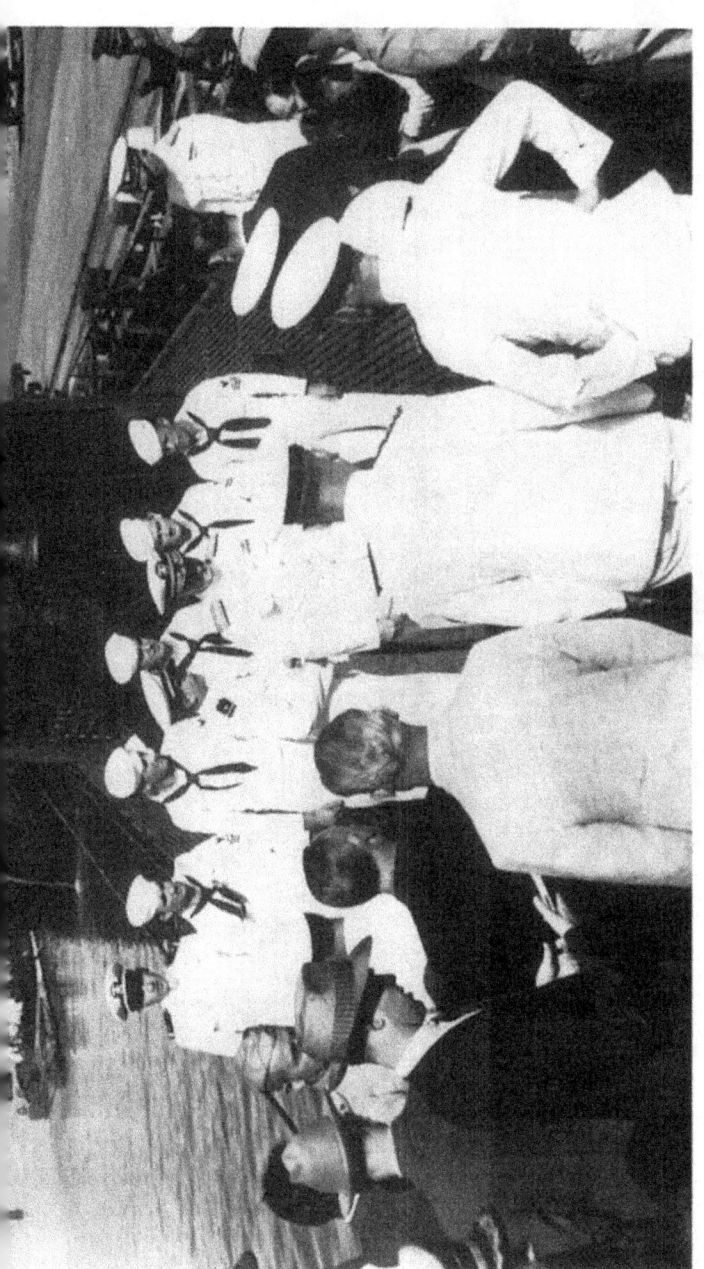

ADMIRAL NIMITZ taking command of the Pacific fleet on board the U.S.S. Grayling, December 31, 1941.

— *Official U.S. Navy photo, Courtesy Captain Roy C. Smith III, USNR (Ret.)*

ADMIRAL NIMITZ shown in the rose garden in his home in Berkeley, California, where he settled after going on inactive duty.
— *Courtesy Admiral Nimitz State Historical Park*

JIMBO EASTWOOD, son of Commander and Mrs. James Eastwood, salutes Fleet Admiral Nimitz on his 75th birthday.
— *Official U.S. Navy photo.*
Courtesy Admiral Nimitz State Historical Park

ADMIRAL NIMITZ shown with his sister, Mrs. Dora Reagon, on April 20, 1948 as he arrived in San Antonio, Texas to attend the San Jacinto Festival.
— *Photo by San Antonio Light, courtesy Admiral Nimitz Center, Fredericksburg, Texas*

ACKNOWLEDGMENTS

When it became known that young Chester Nimitz might attend the U.S. Naval Academy at Annapolis, Maryland, the effort to help him prepare for his entrance examinations became a community project. The pride of the German people in the Texas Hill Country was at stake and those with the ability to teach him were anxious to help.

The same has been true of this publication. Friends in Texas have been joined by former staff members and navy personnel to help prepare an accurate picture of one of the most respected leaders in our history.

One key to the preparation of this book is Douglass Hubbard, superintendent of the Admiral Nimitz State Historical Park in Fredericksburg, Texas. He and his staff have cooperated in every way possible. Mr. Hubbard has made available material — printed matter, tapes, and photographs — that otherwise would have taken years to assemble. He has read the manuscript for content and has written a foreword for the book. Without Douglass Hubbard's encouragement and help, the book would have taken much longer to write.

Thanks must also go to Rear Admiral Ernest M. Eller, USN (Ret.), a member of the Nimitz staff at Pearl Harbor. This noted writer and historian has edited the manuscript for historical accuracy and his "I was there" evaluation of the war in the Pacific leaves little room for argument.

He has written an introduction to the book that

should provide a sober warning to our current leaders — and those in the future.

Without question, Nimitz's original biographer, E. B. Potter, and his classic work helped guide us through the chronology of his life. In a real sense his efforts supplied the prototype for our efforts. For this and his gracious encouragement to see the life of Nimitz further popularized we are extremely grateful.

Captain Roy C. Smith III, USNR (Ret.) of the U.S. Naval Academy Alumni Association, has suggested factual changes that have strengthened the book. He has supplied photographs of the Naval Academy — then and now — as well as a number of desirable shots that are not available in Fredericksburg.

Admiral Charles C. Kirkpatrick, USN (Ret.) of Kerrville, Texas, was a member of the Nimitz staff at Pearl Harbor and has passed on several accounts dealing with his experiences that involved his fellow Texan. The warmth of the Nimitz personality can be seen from the Kirkpatrick stories.

Through the years William J. Lawson of Austin and his wife, Ella, have encouraged us to do this book. Mrs. Lawson, a first cousin to Chester Nimitz, has related accounts of their grandfather, Charles W. Nimitz, that are as humorous as they are heartwarming.

Dr. Gordon Casad of Dallas has helped in research, editing, and in the preparation of the manuscript. Some of our material used has resulted from his suggestions.

The authors are indebted to William E. Dozier, Jr., publisher of the Kerrville *Daily Times* and Mr. and Mrs. Art Kowert of the Fredericksburg *Standard*. Their verbal accounts and newspaper articles are valuable additions to the story.

Adelia Neu of Austin and Barbara Wilson of Round Rock have helped in the preparation of the manuscript. Mrs. Neu did editorial work in the preliminary stages and Mrs. Wilson typed the final manuscript and proofread it.

There are others, too numerous to mention, who have helped with the book. It has been, as previously stated, a cooperative effort.

Frank A. Driskill
Dede W. Casad

BIBLIOGRAPHY

Bennett, Geoffrey, *Naval Battles of World War II*, David Mackay Company, Inc., New York, 1975

Blair, Clay, Jr., *Silent Victory: The U.S. Submarine War Against Japan*, J.B. Lippincott, Co., New York, 1975.

Blassingame, Wyatt, *The Navy's Fliers in World War II*, The Westminster Press, Philadelphia, 1967.

Buell, Thomas B., *The Quite Warrior: A Biography of Raymond A. Spruance*, Little, Brown and Co., Boston, 1974.

Davis, Burke, *Get Yamamoto*, Random House, New York, 1969.

Driskill, Frank A. and Noel Grisham, *The Guide to Historic San Antonio and the Texas Border Country*, Eakin Press, Burnet, 1982.

____, *Historic Churches of Texas*, Eakin Press, Burnet, Texas 1980.

Ewing, William H., *Nimitz: Reflections on Pearl Harbor*, The Admiral Nimitz Foundation, Fredericksburg, Texas, 1971.

Griffith, Samuel B. II, *The Battle for Guadalcanal*, J.B. Lippincott Co., Philadelphia, 1963.

Frank, Benis M., *Okinawa: The Great Island Battle*, Elseview Dutton, New York, 1978.

Halsey, Fleet Admiral William F. & Lieutenant Commander J. Bryan, III, *Admiral Halsey's Story*, McGraw Hill, New York, 1947.

Hoehling, A. A., *The Lexington Goes Down*, Prentice-Hall, New York, 1971.

Hoyt, Edwin P., *How They Won the War in the Pacific: Nimitz and His Admirals*, Weybright and Talley, New York, 1970.

Jordon, Gilbert, *German Texana*, Eakin Press, Burnet, 1981

Kowert, Elise, *Old Homes and Buildings of Fredericksburg*, Fredericksburg Publishing, Fredericksburg, Texas, 1977.

Lamar, H. Arthur, *I Saw Stars*, The Admiral Nimitz Foundation, Fredericksburg, Texas, 1975.

Leckie, Robert, *Challenge for the Pacific*, Doubleday and Company, New York, 1963.

Lord, Walter, *Incredible Victory*, Harper & Row, New York, 1967.

Manchester, William, *Goodbye Darkness*, Little Brown, Boston, 1979.

____, *American Caesar*, Little Brown & Company, Boston, 1978.

Merrill, James M., *A Sailor's Admiral*, Thomas Y. Crowell, Co., New York, 1976.

Morison, Samuel Eliot, *The Two Ocean War*, The Atlantic

Monthly Press Book, Little Brown, and Company, Boston, 1963.
———, *History of the United States Naval Operations in World War II*, 15 Vols. Little Brown and Company, Boston, 1947-62.
Sister Joan of Arc, *My Name is Nimitz*, San Antonio.
Nimitz, Chester W., *Thoughts to Live By*, Fredericksburg, Texas 1981.
Navy Times, *Operation Victory*, G.P. Putman's Sons, New York, 1968.
Newcomb, Richard, *Iwo Jima*, Holt-Rinehart and Winston, New York, 1965.
Nichols, Charles S. Jr., *Okinawa: Victory in the Pacific*, Charles E. Tuttle Co., 1955.
Potter, E.B., *Nimitz*, Naval Institute Press, Annapolis, Maryland, 1976.
———, and Chester W. Nimitz, *The Great Sea War*, Prentice-Hall, Inc., Englewood Cliffs, New Jersey, 1960.
Ryan, Cornelius, *The Longest Day*, Simon & Schuster, New York, 1959.
Steinberg, Rafael, *Island Fighting*, Time/Life, Alexandria, Virginia, 1978.
Stokesbury, James L., *A Short History of World War II*, William Morrow, Co., New York, 1980.
Time/Life, *The Road to Tokyo*, World War II, Alexandria, Virginia.
Toepperwein, Herman, *Steamboat Hotel, A Story of a Frontier Inn*, The Admiral Nimitz Foundation, 1972.

Articles: "Nimitz Fires When He is Ready," *The Rotarian*, April, 1943. "Nimitz and His Admiral's," Harper's Magazine, Feb. 1945. "Miracle At Midway," Reader's Digest, Nov. 1972. "Admiral Chester W. Nimitz," Noel Busch, *Life*, July, 1944; "Swords into Plowshares, Some of Fleet Admiral Nimitz's Lesser Known Contributions to Peace," E.M. Eller, Shipmate, Feb. 1961. Stars and Stripes, J.E. Fisher, "Admiral Nimitz Lives Amid Memories, But Keeps Looking Ahead," Lew Scarr, Copley News Service; "Nimitz" Gilbert Cant, Asia and the Americans, July 1945. "Admiral Nimitz Views Central Asia," Kip Cooper, Copley News Service, 1962. The Southern California Navy Journal, Oct. 1947. Congressional Records, Dec. 15, 1947. "Brain Center," George S. Jones, New York Times Magazine, April 9, 1945. "My Way of Life," Boy's Life, Jan. 1966.

Newspapers: *Alameda Times Star*, Sept. 2, 1954; *Fredericksburg Standard*, Dec. 25, 1941; *The San Diego Union*, March 8, 1953; Feb. 3, 1961; Oct. 28, 1947; June 23, 1960; June 2, 1963; Oct. 25, 1947; Feb. 9, 1963. *The San Francisco Chronicle*, Feb. 18, 1960; Sept. 1, 1954; Feb. 21, 1960. *The Dallas Morning News*, Nov. 11, 1945; Sept. 2, 1962. *San Bernardino Sun*, Oct. 3, 1946. *The Wilkes Barre Record*, Wilkes Barre Pa., Oct. 15, 1947; *The New York Sun*, Oct. 9, 1945; *The Washington Daily News*, Feb. 10, 1944. *San Diego Tribune*, Oct. 27, 1947. *The New York Tribune*, Oct. 10, 1948. *The Austin American*, April 17, 1961. *Los Angeles Times*, July 3, 1960. *New York Time Magazine*, Feb. 29, 1944; April 9, 1945. *Los Angeles Times*, July 3, 1945. *San Diego Tribune*, Oct. 27, 1947. *The Radio Post*, Fredericksburg, Oct. 11, 1945. *Business Machines*, Oct. 16, 1945. *The New York Times*, Oct. 6, 7, 1945. *The Arizona Daily Star*, Oct. 16, 1947.

INDEX

Abilene, Tex., 199
Adenauer, Konrad, 277
Akagi, 158, 162, 163
Alabama, 155
Annapolis, Md., 51, 54, 80, 89, 113, 284, 289
Arizona, 102, 131, 132
Arnold, H. H., 213
Atlanta, 177
Augusta, 99
Austin, Tex., 10, 29, 199, 250, 253

Baltimore, 72, 75
Bassett, Prentice, 83, 84, 87
Batangas Harbor, 78-80
Beecher, William Gordon, Jr., 243
Bellinger, Patrick, 135
Berkeley, Cal., 96, 230, 270, 272, 282
Bertolette, Levi Calvin, 57
Brisbane, Austral., 174, 201, 202, 207
Briscoe, Dolph, 77
Brown, Wilson, 58
Brutus, 197

Calhoun, William L., 142
Canaga, Bruce, 65, 70, 72, 73, 99
Carpender, Arthur S., 171
Carter, Glenn Owen, 79
Casad, Gordon, 290
Catarina, Tex., 77
Cavite, 75
Charleston, S.C., 9
Chicago, Ill., 125
Church, Albert, 61, 62
Churchill, Winston, 208, 209, 265, 266
Civil War, 16, 29, 156
Clarendon, Tex., 199
Cleveland, O., 89
Coronet, 225
Cruikshank, William H., 46

Dallas, Tex., 196, 247-249
Decatur, 75, 78, 79, 81, 124, 267
Denfeld, Louis E., 260, 269, 273
Denver, 79
Dewey, George, 55, 72
    Thomas E., 206
Dexter, Al, 194
Doolittle, James H., 185, 212
Dozier, William E., Jr., 290

Draemel, Milo, 58
Drake, William Waldo, 259
Duke of York, 212

Easter fires, 25, 27
Eastwood, James, 287
    Jimbo, 287
Eisenhower, Dwight D., 67, 171, 213, 233, 262
El Paso, Tex., 12, 33
Eller, Ernest M., 280, 286, 289
Enterprise, 147, 148, 156, 161
Ewing, Bill, 112

Fairlong, William P., 97
Fitch, Aubrey W., 58, 142, 170
Fletcher, Fred, 58, 147, 156, 158, 161, 171, 173
Forrestal, James, 217, 233, 234, 240-242, 245, 246, 257, 259, 261-264, 275
Frazer, Bruce, 209, 212
Fredericksburg, Tex., 3-5, 10, 12, 14, 15, 19, 22, 25, 29-31, 33-35, 37, 38, 42, 44, 53, 56, 88, 90, 199, 250, 251, 253, 254, 257, 277, 280, 283, 289-290
Freeman, Catherine (see Nimitz, Catherine)
    Elizabeth, 84, 85, 87, 89
    Robert, 84, 85
Friedrich, Prince, 3
Fukuoka, 266

Gallaher, Dan, 235
Galvanic, 188, 189
Garden of Peace, 280
Germany, 7, 8
Ghormley, Robert L., 58, 142, 171, 173-176
Gilbert Islands, 146, 188, 189, 191
Gillespie Rifles, 16, 29, 78
Grayling, 138, 165
Groton, Conn., 100
Guadalcanal, 169, 170, 173-177, 179, 181, 185
Guam, 153, 215-217, 219, 221, 224, 229

Halsey, William F., 58-60, 75, 115, 146-148, 156, 176, 185, 187, 207, 227, 228, 244, 272

Hamburg, Ger., 90
Harmon, ___, 171
Harris, U.R., 75
Hartford, 66
Hawkins, Charles E., 196, 197
   William D., 196
Heiser, Lester A., 59, 60
Henke, Dorthea 2, 4, 15, 32, 90
   Heinrich, 2, 4, 12, 15, 38, 42
Henry, O., 31
Hewitt, Kent, 58
Hiei, 177
Hinkamp, Clarence, 84, 85, 88
Hiroshima, 226
Hiryu, 158, 164
Holland, 80
Holmes, Jasper, 155
Honolulu, 95, 96, 190, 199
Hornet, 161, 162
Hosogaya, Boshiro, 158
Houston, 198
Houston, Tex., 199
Hubbard, Douglass, 289

Indiana, 69
Indianapolis, 100, 267
Indianola, 8, 10, 12
Independence, 197
Ingersall, Royal, 58, 63, 65
Invincible, 197
Iwo Jima, 207, 216, 217, 219

Jacobs, Randall, 123, 124
Johnson, Lyndon B., 78, 172, 250, 276
Juneau, 177

Kaga, 158, 164
Kalinin Bay, 212
Kashmir, 273-275
Kerrville, Tex., 22, 36-38, 40, 43-45, 88, 90, 199, 250-253
Kidd, Isaac, 131, 132
Kimmel, Husband, 58, 109, 110, 127, 132, 135, 137, 138, 151, 153
Kincaid, Thomas C., 58
King, Ernest, 57, 75, 125, 133, 145, 146, 148, 170-175, 182-185, 190, 204, 208, 209, 213, 225-227, 235, 241, 242, 257, 262
Kirkpatrick, Charles C., 141, 290
Knights of the Sword, 7
Knights of the Teutonic Order, 7
Knox, Frank, 107, 109, 110, 123, 125, 217, 259

Koo, Wellington, 232
Kowert, Art, 290
Kruger, Jack B., 247

LaGuardia, Fiorello, 242-243
Lamar, Hal Arthur, 106, 125, 127, 130-133, 202, 218, 228, 235
Lawson, William J. and Ella, 80, 290
Layton, Edwin T., 151, 152, 154-157, 159, 161-162, 164-166, 185, 225, 227
Leahy, William D., 192, 213
Leary, Fairfax, 58, 65
Lee, Robert E., 31
Lexington, 148, 156, 170
Lie, Trygve, 276
Livonia, 7
Logan, Leavitt C., 70, 72
Longstreet, James, 31
Los Angeles, Cal., 133

MacArthur, Douglas, 118, 130, 144, 148, 170-175, 181-183, 192, 196, 200-207, 213, 215, 218, 219, 223-224, 227-229, 234, 258, 259
Makalapa, 137, 187, 207
Manila Bay, 69, 75, 78
Marshall, George C., 167, 171, 184, 189, 204, 205, 213, 258, 262
Marshall Islands, 146, 188
Maryland, 120
Massachusetts, 69
Matagorda Bay, 8
Maumee, 92-94
McCain, John S., 58, 170, 171
McKnight, Felix, 247, 250
McVay, Charles, 267
Mercer, Preston, 172
Meusebach, Ottfried Hans von, 4, 10, 11, 25, 27
Midway, 119, 149, 151, 154-159, 161-165, 167, 168, 170, 172, 173
Mikasa, 279, 281
Miller, Harold B., 250
   Sam, 43-44
Mindanao, 73-74
Missouri, 160, 228, 229, 234, 249, 256, 257, 279
Mitchell, ___, 186
Mobile, Ala., 197
Moore, H.A., 253
   Susan, 17, 52, 253
Mueller, Lisetta, 17

Index 297

Muller, Sophie Dorthea, 10
Musashi, 186

Nagasaki, 226
Nagumo, Chuichi, 158, 159, 162, 163
Narwhal, 83, 86
Navy Register, 109
Nehru, Jawaharlal, 275
Neu, Adelia, 290-291
New Braunfels, Tex., 4, 8, 10
New Orleans, La., 197
New York, N.Y., 89, 91, 233, 234, 242, 243, 247, 257, 258, 276
Newton, John H., 79
Ney, Elizabet, 31
Nicholas, 228
Nimitz, 129
NIMITZ, Anna Henke, 4, 5, 7, 13, 14, 21, 35-37, 39, 40, 43, 54, 61, 88, 90, 94
   Anna "Nancy", 95, 97, 269
   Catherine Freeman, 72, 83-91, 94, 97, 99, 100, 105, 123, 124, 132, 178, 200, 219, 229, 235, 250, 268, 269, 272, 278
   Catherine Vance "Kate", 91, 97, 126, 268
   Charles Bernard, 13, 14, 40
   Charles Henry (Captain) (Opa), 4-7, 14-18, 21, 22, 24, 27-29, 31-33, 35, 44-46, 50, 51, 53, 54, 57, 62, 65, 67, 69, 72-74, 77, 80, 81, 88, 125, 281
   Charles Henry, Jr., 14
   Chester Jr. (Chet), 91, 97, 99, 100, 129, 240, 268, 278
   Dora (Reagon), 36, 39, 42, 61, 92, 235, 254, 288
   Karl (cousin), 24
   Karl Heinrich, Jr., 8, 9
   Karl Heinrich, Sr., 8, 10
   Mary Mason, 97, 200, 235, 268
   "Oma", 15, 22
   Otto, 36, 42, 61, 88, 252
   William (Willie), 14, 35, 36, 52-54, 61, 90
Norfolk, Va., 234
North Dakota, 85
Nürnberg, Ger., 90

Ohio, 65, 69, 70-72, 75, 100
Ohnishi, ___, 211
Okinawa, 207, 211, 216, 218-220, 222, 223

Oklahoma, 120
Olympic, 225
Operation Magic Carpet, 257

Panay, 73-76
Paragua, 73
Pauley, Edwin, 259-261
Pearl Harbor, 55, 57, 95, 96, 105-107, 109, 110, 111, 114, 122-124, 127, 131-133, 138, 151, 152, 154, 157-159, 166, 172, 175, 179, 181-184, 186, 187, 191, 200, 201, 204, 209, 211, 215, 217-219, 229, 249, 257, 259, 262
Pedernales River, 20, 255
Percival, Arthur, 228
Perry, Matthew Calbraith, 228
   Oliver H., 164
Philippines, 119, 181, 183, 203, 204, 208, 215
Pickard, Carl, 43-44
Plunger, 82, 98
Poland, 7-8
Polloc, 73-74
Port Arthur, Tex., 94
Porter, David Dixon, 156
Portland, 177
Portsmouth, Treaty of, 72, 74
Potter, E. B., 290
Pye, William, 57, 110, 127, 135, 137, 138, 149

Quincy, Mass., 83, 84

Ranger, 79
Regal, 99
Richardson, J.O., 101, 188, 189, 193, 204, 205
Rigel, 86
Riley, Bertha, 39
Roberts, Owen J., 127
Robison, Samuel S., 94-96, 128
Rochefort, Joseph J., 152-155, 159, 162, 166
Rodzinski, Arthur, 105
Roosevelt, E., 31
   Eleanor, 187-188, 225
   Franklin Delano, 106, 109, 115, 125, 125, 127, 133, 175, 187, 192, 200, 204-206, 208, 209, 218, 225, 259
   Theodore, 55, 71, 72, 76, 115
Rosenthal, Joe, 216
Rusk, Dean, 277

Ryan, Walter O., 187

St. Charles Hotel, 36-37, 40, 44
St. Louis, 212
St. Louis, Mo., 54, 94
San Angelo, Tex., 25
San Antonio, Tex., 33, 43, 45, 46, 53, 54, 65, 99, 199, 288
San Diego, Cal., 12, 97, 99, 100, 133
San Francisco, Cal., 65, 100, 154, 157, 172, 182, 217, 229, 232, 235, 271, 277
San Jacinto, 198
Sangamon, 212
Santa Anna, 197
Santee, 212
Saratoga, 147
Sargo, 100
Schreiner, Louis, 39
Shafroth, John F., 106
Sheridan, Philip, 31
Sherman, Forrest P., 182, 235, 250, 276
Skipjack, 83, 85, 88
Slaydon, James, 46, 47, 51, 52, 54, 65
Smith, H.M., 113, 184, 188, 189, 219
   Julian, 191
   Roy C., 290
   William, 135
Solomons, 170, 171, 175, 176, 178
Soryu, 158, 164
Spruance, Raymond A., 58, 75, 156, 158, 61, 164, 184, 191, 207, 211, 266
Stark, Harold, 58, 106, 125
Stevenson, Coke, 221, 250
Stewart, C.V., 63
   George, 89
Stonewall, Tex., 78
Sturgeon, 84, 85, 88
Sullivan, John L., 272
Suwanee, 212
Sweden, 7

Taft, Charles, 76
   William Howard, 76-77
Takasu, Shiru, 158
Talbot, 98
Texas Hill Country, 3, 10, 45, 55, 69, 93, 253, 254, 276, 277, 289
Texas Rangers, 10
Tivy Cemetery, 41
Tivy High School (Kerrville), 40
Tivy, Joseph, 40
Tivy, Mountain, 40-42, 51-54, 128, 255

Tivy, Suson, 40-42
Togo, Heihachiro, 70, 71, 74, 99, 279, 280, 283
Tojo, Hideki, 182
Toland, John G., 52, 245, 253
Towers, John H., 58, 142, 241
Train, Harold C., 135
Trenton, 100
Truman, Harry S, 214, 225, 227, 234, 236, 239, 257-259, 261, 262, 264, 265, 269, 272, 273, 275
Tsushima, 70, 99, 279
Turner, Richard Kelly, 58, 171, 174, 176, 77, 184, 188

U.S. Naval Academy, 47, 51, 52, 55-57, 60, 62, 65, 67, 72, 83, 284, 289
Univ. of California, 96
Upton, ___, 99
Ushijima, Mitsuru, 220, 222

Vandergrift, A.A., 171, 174-176, 219, 273

Wadsworth, Alexander, 79
Wainwright, Jonathan, 228, 233
Wake Island, 119, 135, 137, 138, 154, 156, 164, 180
Washington, D.C., 54, 90, 94, 99, 102, 105, 107, 109, 124, 129, 133, 148, 152, 169-171, 173, 174, 181, 182, 185, 200, 202, 215, 218, 223, 233-239, 241, 245, 259, 261, 263, 265, 272, 273
Watchtower, 170, 171, 173, 176, 178
Watson, Thomas J., 270
Werntz Preparatory School, 55
West Point, 46, 67
Westervelt, William T., 46
White Plains, 212
Willkie, Wendell, 206
Wilson, Barbara, 290, 291
Wollaston, Mass., 84, 88, 90
Woodson, W.B., 101
Worcester, Poly. Inst., 14
Wright, Elizabeth, 195

Yamamoto, Osoroku, 151, 152, 154, 156-158, 161, 164, 169, 173, 185, 186, 235
Ykasaki, ___, 232
Yorktown, 147, 148, 160-162, 165

Zion Lutheran Church (Fredericksburg), 15

www.ingramcontent.com/pod-product-compliance
Lightning Source LLC
Chambersburg PA
CBHW071655160426
43195CB00012B/1478